Marketing Ideas
for the Small Business

Marketing Ideas for the Small Business

P. W. and P. F. Sterrett

MERCURY

First published in 1989
by Mercury Books

Published in paperback 1990
by Mercury Books
Gold Arrow Publications Ltd
862 Garratt Lane, London SW17 0NB

Set in Plantin by Avocet Robinson, Buckingham
Printed and bound in Great Britain by
Mackays of Chatham PLC, Chatham, Kent

British Library Cataloguing in Publication Data

Sterrett, P.W.
  Marketing ideas for the small business
  1. Marketing by small firms – Manuals
  I. Title   II. Sterrett, P.F.
  658.8

  ISBN 1–85252–049–3

CONTENTS

CONTENTS

PREFACE

by

Paddy Sterrett

By the age of twenty, I knew I had a gift for devising unusual games and competitions, and I was for ever being asked to help raise money for charity. At the age of twenty-five, I began to consider work in the marketing and promotions field. I was confident of my abilities, but found that firms were unwilling to employ me because I had no training in this field. Eventually, in desperation, I decided to borrow money and 'go it alone!'

It was not easy to obtain my first contract, but finally, determination and perseverance won the day and I convinced a well-known firm in Northern Ireland that I was capable of launching their new confectionery product on the market. It was vital that this first promotion be a big success if I was to make any progress, for in the marketing field you are only as good as your last success. One flop and you are on the way out! Luckily, I was able to devise a promotional campaign that immediately appealed to the public and the firm reported a big increase in turnover. From then on my progress was easy. Promotional agencies and the management of firms up and down the country turned to me. People would ask me to come up with unusual, out-of-the-ordinary and exciting new promotional ideas, and I gradually made a name for myself.

Over the years I have been acquainted with many owners of small firms who have been desperate to promote their goods and to increase their turnover in business. They could not afford the cost of fees for professional marketing and promotional campaigns, and so they had resigned themselves to defeat. The idea of promoting their own firms had never really entered their heads!

When I encouraged them to start a promotional campaign of their own, they were horrified at first. But many, after a little guidance and encouragement, managed very successfully after I had told them how to set about it. To their surprise and delight, the schemes did not cost them a lot to put into operation, the work involved did not tax their skills to an intolerable degree and neither did it take up a phenomenal amount of time. And, most important, their efforts were successful.

Contrary to popular belief, there are NOT a lot of secret techniques to learn. People do NOT need specialist skills to operate a highly successful promotion, and neither do they need vast capital reserves. Novices have proved again and again that they can achieve incredible results on a very modest budget.

When, after a lengthy and successful career in the promotions and marketing field, I was forced to retire owing to ill-health, I was able to fulfil a long-held ambition and commit my experience to paper. With the help and encouragement of my wife, Patricia, and all her hard work in collating, deciphering my notes, and writing, this book is the result. It describes in detail the operation of a range of promotional ideas which can be undertaken by entrepreneurs who own their own small business and who cannot afford the vast amounts charged by professional firms. The promotions are all fairly easy for the average person to undertake. They need only a very moderate outlay and have all proved highly successful in the past. By following the guidelines, you will avoid possible pitfalls and develop the confidence to undertake the sorts of venture you would never have dared tackle before.

So, read on, and good luck! We wish you all success. If you follow the instructions, we are confident that you will enjoy your new activity and find it rewarding from every point of view.

Part 1

DOING IT YOURSELF: THE ADVANTAGES

1

PROMOTIONAL ENTERPRISE

Promotional enterprise has become big business today. Advertisements on radio and television capture our imagination and bring new products into our homes. Large, colourful advertisements in newspapers and magazines describe the attributes of all the latest products on the market. Impressive, glossy, colour pamphlets and brochures get pushed through our letter boxes every day, and we cannot but be amazed by the offers of vast fortunes, fabulous prizes, massive cash discounts and special offers that wealthy firms can offer their customers. In this age of high technology, promotional ventures are becoming more exciting and more innovative every year. Experts are forever finding fascinating new ways to attract customers, and the more unusual the gimmick, the more successful it tends to be.

Multinational firms can afford exotic promotions on a vast scale. They can also offer extravagant and highly desirable prizes for the winners of promotional games and competitions. The high cost of planning, administering, advertising and organising an impressive national publicity campaign presents no problem. And they can sell goods more cheaply too, as they purchase equipment in massive quantities, thus reducing their costs. They can also manufacture and deliver goods more cheaply when they operate in bulk quantities.

[3]

This is why owners of small firms often feel so inadequate. They know that they can never compete on that sort of scale. But think about the phrase 'Marketing and Promotions'. It might conjure up a picture of extravagantly expensive and highly professional promotional expertise, but the *New Oxford Dictionary* tells us that 'Marketing' means: 'A method of selling or disposing of goods or services', and the emphasis is quite rightly on the word 'method'. Ten different people can sell the same quality product or service and offer the same value for money, yet because they all use different selling techniques, some will report a much higher turnover than others. And success is not dependent on size. It is those who employ the best promotional methods to sell their product who attract the most customers and so sell more goods and achieve greater profits.

To illustrate the importance of good promotional ideas when selling a product, let me describe an exercise that was conducted by a garden centre whose management decided to attract customers by promoting a new type of wheelbarrow. They engaged three different promotional schemes and then compared the success of the ventures.

For the first promotion they employed a well-known marketing and consultant agency, who charged an exorbitant fee for their services and expected a percentage of the profits. The professional company organised a crossword competition, which could be entered into by all those who purchased a wheelbarrow. For a prize they offered an exotic holiday abroad for two people. The winner would be the person who, having submitted a correct entry to the competition, had their name drawn from a drum in which all the other winning entries had been placed. The draw was to take place in the garden centre on the last day of the competition.

The competition was well planned and those who were paying the consultants waited eagerly for a record rise in the sale of wheelbarrows. They had invested a lot of money in the promotion and naturally expected phenomenal results.

There were many entries to the competition, but although sales of the wheelbarrow increased, they did not reach anything like the expected target. Fees to the marketing firm, plus the cost of the holiday, plus additional expenses incurred by the promotion drained away 75 per cent of the profit made from the sales of the product. The management were very disillusioned and felt cheated, having expected the wide publicity and the high cost of the operation to ensure a far greater response from the public and guarantee them a far larger profit.

Management learned the hard way that to employ an expensive professional firm and to operate a costly promotional campaign is no guarantee of profit and success.

A second competition was organised later that same year. This was a simple promotion devised and organised by the manager, without the assistance of a marketing and promotions firm.

People were asked to guess, to the nearest ounce, the weight of the wheelbarrow plus a bag of bulbs. All those who purchased a wheelbarrow were entitled to enter, and on the final day of the competition the three people to have guessed nearest to the correct weight won a voucher for £15, to be spent at the centre.

This competition was very popular. It cost very little to organise and yet the sale of wheelbarrows increased dramatically and rose to over 14 per cent more than expected.

The management were well pleased with their efforts, especially as the total cost of administering this promotion came to only 10 per cent of the profit made.

A third promotion proved to be the most successful of all. Not only was it cheap and easy to operate, but it was the most popular, because it offered both excitement and a challenge to the gambling instinct.

Everyone who purchased a wheelbarrow during the three-week promotional period was given a receipt on which were recorded the date and the time of purchase. These details were also recorded on the register.

On the last day of the competition, a member of the public was asked to pick a slip of paper from each of two drum containers. On the first was printed a date, on the second a time. The winner was the customer whose date and time of purchase were nearest to the date and time drawn out of each drum. The winner was given a full refund on the cost of their wheelbarrow.

This was not an exotic prize, but the competition really had customer appeal as it was geared to the clientele. Sales of the wheelbarrows rose to 21 per cent more than the expected average, yet the cost of the promotion came to only a fraction of the percentage of profits.

The organisers liked this competition because it was simple to operate; the customers liked it because, for very little effort, they had a chance of winning a refund on the wheelbarrow that they had needed to buy in the first place, and they enjoyed the anticipation of waiting to see which numbers would be drawn from the drums.

Because the competition was a little bit different, the promotion was an unqualified success from every point of view.

By telling this story, I hope I have illustrated a variety of points. First, it is NOT always the most expensive promotional campaigns that have the widest popular appeal. Second, a promotional campaign does not need to be expensive in order to be successful. Third, often the simple and straightforward games and competitions are the ones that attract the most interest. And finally, modest promotions are capable of stimulating a considerable turnover and profit for the company that uses them.

In many ways the smaller business arranging its own promotions has the advantage over a larger concern employing a professional organisation. Professional firms charge a high fee for devising a specially copyrighted promotional idea for the exclusive use of one particular company. An additional fee must be paid if they are to put their campaign into operation, and this service does not come cheap! This fee will not include extra miscellaneous expenses which cannot be determined in advance, and they can be very costly too. Professional firms often ask for a percentage of whatever profit is made, so the venture has to be an outstanding success before a high profit can be made.

In my opinion, it is those who manufacture or sell the commodity that is being promoted who are in the best position to promote it. They know all about the product, its good points and its weaknesses, and they know its quality and value to the consumer. They are also fully acquainted with details about rival firms that sell similar products and services. With a comprehensive knowledge of the product or service you are trying to sell, half the battle is won. If you have faith in the product, the promotion will somehow reflect your confidence, and you will find yourself answering all the questions a newcomer might ask with conviction.

When I first began my career in marketing and promotions work, I studied the reaction of people to the games and competitions that I had devised to test their skills and amuse them. I discovered that people have many common weaknesses which I could use to advantage when planning promotional campaigns.

1. Everyone loves to feel that they have won something for nothing. If the prize offered is good value for money, it will attract people. A shopping voucher is always popular because the winners can choose goods that they really want.

2. People love a challenge. They like to use their brains to work out solutions to problems, especially when they have as much chance as anyone else of winning a good prize.

3. People love to play exciting games that stimulate the mind and the imagination and which bring a little amusement and fun into their lives.

[7]

4. People love to gamble. This is a fact of life, even though some people choose not to recognise it. This is why competitions that appeal to the gaming instinct are always popular.

5. People are very competitive and they love to pit 'their wits against other people. They feel a real sense of pride and achievement if they win.

For all these reasons guessing games, quizzes and puzzles are popular pastimes for many people, as are unusual games and competitions that challenge the wit and skill of the players. Any promotion which takes these points into account has a fair chance of being successful.

So, don't be defeated by thoughts of ingenious and costly promotions that the world of big business can indulge in. As a small operator you can attract all the customers you need by operating a modest and simple promotional scheme. But don't take my word for it. Choose one of the promotions in this book and find out for yourself. You will be glad that you did!

Part 2

HOW TO DO IT

2

HAVE CONFIDENCE
– It Can Be Done

You might well be aware that a good promotion can draw attention to your wares, but without experience in this field you may feel reluctant to experiment and test your skills.

Once again I must emphasise the point. You do NOT need special skills to operate a successful promotion. Nor do you need massive capital resources. You will attract people to your firm very effectively once you have learned some of the basic 'tricks of the trade' outlined in this book. A smaller-scale, simple-to-operate promotion, which most people would not be afraid to tackle, often has more public appeal than a larger, more elaborate and costly undertaking.

Do follow the instructions carefully, though. Although you might be tempted to add variations of your own and take short cuts, this is not recommended. It is the procedures as outlined which have proved to be the most successful in operation. If you deviate from the recommended procedure, you may fall into unexpected pitfalls that will mar the efficiency and effectiveness of your campaign.

Each promotional idea may be suitable for two or three different types of retail outlet. You can provide that personal touch that makes each one just that little bit special, for it is the personal touch that makes the difference between an ordinary promotion and a very successful one.

Once you have had a good response from your public and achieved a significant increase in turnover and profit, you will never look back. You will feel confident in your ability to try as many of the schemes as you wish – always with the same degree of success.

Owners of small family firms are often afraid of falling victim to what seems to be 'unfair' competition from large national and multinational companies. When you are operating on a limited budget, problems can seem insurmountable if a branch of a vast, wealthy organisation opens up on the doorstep. This is especially true at the start, when the new 'super firm' is trying to get established. Its management, in an endeavour to attract customers, will offer special discounts on goods which members of the public just cannot resist. Competition on this scale can cause despair to smaller firms in the same neighbourhood, especially when they sell the same types of goods and provide similar services.

If you are faced with a dilemma like this, a lot will depend on your character, your determination and will to succeed, your faith in yourself and your business expertise and skill.

Sometimes people are so paralysed by fear that they are unable to take any positive action. Those who dwell on the negative aspects of competition often make themselves ill and depressed. They convince themselves that there is nothing that they can do, and because of this attitude they are defeated from the start.

Some drift along, providing the same service with no improvements, in spite of the severe competition. These people depend on the loyalty of their few remaining customers, and if they eke out a living they are fortunate. Obviously they have to accept a lower standard of living as a result.

Some entrepreneurs, finding that their turnover has fallen rapidly in a very short space of time, take panic action without thinking the problem through. In desperation, they sell up at a loss because sales are so low and they are afraid of going bankrupt. Others are faced with the reality of bankruptcy and liquidation.

These are heartbreaking experiences, especially for those who have previously enjoyed their work and been happy and secure. Those who have never been in debt before may be stunned by the experience. Some spend the rest of their lives trying to recover.

Often situations like these would not have occurred if the crisis had been tackled correctly. A fall in turnover will obviously cause problems if the matter is allowed to continued, but I have proved many times that you can overcome the challenge of fierce competition if you channel your energies in the right direction and in the right frame of mind.

Fear of bankruptcy is often unfounded and can usually be lifted if only sufficient thought and planning are given to finding a solution to the problem. The first step is to stop resigning yourself to fate and to the conviction that nothing can be done. You should never allow yourself to succumb to the injustices of life. Instead, you should think positively and take the following steps to try to resolve the situation.

1. Make an effort to discover ways in which you can attract customers to your business.

2. Think of ways in which you can increase turnover and profit margins to a level that has never been achieved before.

3. Do a little research on the NEEDS of people living in the area.

4. Find out, by use of a questionnaire, what gaps there are in the services being provided at present and discover which products and services are most in demand.

5. Decide which particular service you would best be able to supply.

6. Once you are ready to start your new venture, advertise its availability at your business.

7. Promote your new venture by using one of the schemes outlined in this book. This will draw attention to your product or service in a most acceptable way.

When faced with serious competition, you need no longer accept defeat. Look closely at your situation and take action to remedy the problem. This may seem difficult, but IT CAN BE DONE. There are always gaps in the services provided for people in the community. It is up to you to identify them and decide which you are best able to fill.

3

WHAT'S GOING WRONG?
– *The Questionnaire*

Those who begin to suffer from reduced profits should quickly ask themselves the following questions:

1. Where am I falling down in my market?

2. What are my competitors offering that proves so attractive to customers?

3. What am I going to do about it?

4. What commodity or service should I sell to bring customers back?

5. What promotional idea shall I undertake to draw attention to my store?

If you are going to find solutions, you must take time to provide honest answers to these questions. One very effective way to obtain the information needed is to draw up a QUESTIONNAIRE to be completed by members of the general public. Encourage people to take part by offering a £1 DISCOUNT on the purchase of goods valued at £6 or more for those who co-operate.

The questionnaire could be delivered to households in the area with a request that the form be returned to the store, or you could visit at least 250 homes and ask people the questions in person. This is the best way, for those interviewed are more likely then to become your first new clients!

Once you receive the answers to your questions, you can soon determine what improvements or innovations the public would like to see made, and you can decide realistically which service or commodity will bring customers flooding back through the doors.

The price of a product or service is not always the main attraction to customers. There are other equally important considerations: value for money, prompt and efficient service and a cheery smile and helpful manner are all ingredients vital to success.

Before drawing up your questionnaire there are various factors to consider.

Compare Prices

Grocers should compare the cost of an average week's groceries purchased from a supermarket with the cost of the same items in their shop. The difference, after travelling expenses and car-parking facilities have been taken into account and deducted, is the amount around which plans for promotional and marketing activity can be devised.

Cost Of Travel

It is important to research the cost of travelling for customers who have to make long journeys to large supermarkets in order to purchase goods. The cost of this transport can eat into the savings made on goods, even if they were purchased at bargain prices! In one case, calculations revealed that goods bought for

£40 from a supermarket some distance away showed a net savings of only 13.5 pence when petrol and running costs were taken into account.

The major motoring organisations will give you the average car fuel consumption costs per mile, and it is quite a sobering thought that if a person has to travel two miles further to buy cheaper petrol, the cost of the journey may eat away up to 60 per cent of the savings made. The only way to make a clear profit is when one has to travel to the vicinity of the cut-price firm on other business!

Time Factor

The time it takes to make the journey to a cut-price firm should also be taken into consideration. Time is a precious commodity today and should be part of the equation when you are assessing the value of a service to the community. People spending time travelling can usually be more usefully and more profitably employed in other ways, and this is where the local store can score points if it offers a worthwhile service.

With these thoughts in mind, you can now draw up your questionnaire. List prices and show the advantages in cash savings on special items in your store and remind potential customers about the many benefits of shopping locally. At the same time, use the questionnaire to advertise the whole range of goods you have for sale.

Word Your Questionnaire Carefully

The wording of questions must be such that answers can be easily collated and used in your assessment of future plans. These answers will give you ideas as to which new products and services would be in demand. Make it clear to householders that this is why you need the information. It may then be possible for you to fill a gap in the market, to the benefit of both you and the householder.

Where possible, word the questionnaire so that short answers only need to be given. Send it out with a covering letter explaining what you hope to achieve. Figure 1 will give you an idea of what you need to do.

Depending on the type of commodity sold in your shop, you will think of other questions that are relevant.

Those who have never undertaken a research project like this may feel a little reticent at first, but there is no reason to feel shy. You should not feel apprehensive about imposing on people in this way because members of the public are usually happy to answer questions, especially when they know that they might benefit in the future from the provision of improved or new services.

Everyman's DIY Store, High Street, West Town

John and Judith Penny invite you to visit their shop in High Street. This is the store where you can find most of the DIY equipment you need for modernising and maintaining your home.

At present we are hoping to develop and improve our existing facilities, and we would like you to help us provide a better service for our customers by answering the following questions.
Your answers will enable us to:

1. determine which goods or services are in most demand.

2. decide how best we can satisfy our customers' needs.

3. assess whether we can provide the goods and services that you require at competitive prices.

We hope that you will oblige us by answering the questionnaire, and if you deliver this form, completed, to the above address, we will be happy to give you a free selection of goods to the value of £1 when you spend £6 or more in the shop.

We look forward to meeting you soon,

John and Judith Penny

QUESTIONNAIRE

1. How much money, approximately, do you spend on DIY materials each month? . . . . .

2. Do you use a car or public transport for shopping? . . . . .

3. How many miles do you travel to go shopping each week? . . . . .

4. Do you shop at Everyman's DIY store? . . . . .

5. When did you last shop at your local DIY store? . . . . .

6. Would you shop locally if the shop offered special incentives? . . . . .

7. What commodities would you like to find for sale in your local shop?
. . . .

8. What services would you like provided that are not available at present? . . . .

9. Which of the following facilities would you use if they were provided at this store?
Hire of carpet shampoo machine . . . . .
Tool hire . . . . .
Key-cutting . . . . .
Wood-cutting service . . . . .
Other . . . .

10. Is time taken in travelling to the shops important to you? . . . . .

11. Does the cost of petrol, plus running costs and wear and tear of a motor car, influence your decision as to where you shop? . . . . .
Bear in mind that the average car costs approximately . . . . . per mile in small town areas and . . . . . in dense traffic.

FIGURE 1.   Sample questionnaire

4

SOUND ADVICE
ABOUT ADVERTISING

Having decided on the item or service that you want to promote, the next step is to choose one of the promotions from this book to bring it to public attention. Choose one which you will enjoy and which will appeal to YOUR public. This is always the first step to success.

Then you must advertise your promotional campaign and let members of the community know when it is going to be launched. Success will depend to some extent on the amount of effort put into advertising and launching your scheme. This is just as important as the presentation and packaging of a product. So the promotion must be brought to the attention of people and it must be made to look attractive and worthwhile.

You therefore need to use all the means at your disposal to advertise your wares locally and tell people about the promotion. The more publicity you give it, the better the response will be.

Advertise In A Local Newspaper

This is an expensive way of advertising but it can be very effective if you do something different to attract the reader. The advert will go unnoticed unless it is displayed to give maximum impact, so think of ways to attract the eye to its position on the page.

To give an advertisement added appeal, use one or more of the following schemes:

1. Allow a discount of 12 per cent of the total purchase on purchases of £5 or more up to a maximum of £2 total discount when customers present the advertisement, cut out of the paper.

2. Incorporate a small coupon in the advertisement. This can then be used as a FREE entry into a competition being run at the store. (Use one of the competitions in this book.)

3. Also offer a FREE draw at the end of a fixed period of time. Advertisement coupons must be returned to the shop showing the contestant's name and address. (Leave space for this information at the bottom of the advertisement.) If the coupon has to be placed in a box at the store, this will bring people into the shop, and few people will enter a shop just to enter a competition. Most will want to have a look around and will hopefully purchase something!

4. Alternatively, incorporate part of a number of well-known slogans or sayings into the advertisement. Invite people to complete the sentence and return the entry form to a box in your shop. The first all-correct entry drawn out of the box on a specified date wins a shopping voucher, redeemable at the store.

This competition should last for approximately three weeks, and the winning name should be drawn by a member of the public either in the shop or in a public place.

Advertising On Posters

Posters should be as large as possible, and they should be colourful and attractive to the eye. The number of posters that you have printed will depend on the number of suitable sites you can find within a radius of five miles from your store.

A4-size posters can be placed inside your store and on the walls outside. Put these adverts on any public noticeboard that you can find. Smaller posters can be put in shop-window displays.

Poster sites in prominent positions are more expensive than others because they are likely to attract more customers and so the competition for them is greater.

When working out your budget for this type of advertising, it is advisable to discuss your requirements with the advertising contractors who operate sites in the area that you wish to cover. They will tell you which sites are available and how much they cost. Poster sites come cheaper when used for a prolonged period of time, say six to eight months, so take this factor into account when planning an advertising campaign.

It helps to employ some form of gimmick when using posters as your advertising medium. A commercial artist could be employed to print some of the wording on the poster upside down or back to front. Alternatively, you could introduce a very obvious spelling mistake. People are naturally curious, and most people like to determine the correct text of an advertisement that is worded oddly. If you use this gimmick, make sure that readers have to decipher the whole of the advertisement before they find out what is being promoted. This game provides a challenge that is difficult to resist, and people who play the game will remember the name of the store and the product more easily because they have put effort into deciphering the words on the poster.

One very successful advertisement for a garden centre read as follows:

WE HAVE TAHW UOY DEEN, EMOC OT SU DNA DNIF TUO TAHW TI SI!
. . . . . . IT WILL BE WORTH YOUR WHILE.

This poster was displayed in two shopping precincts, in two open areas, on main roads and in a coach station. The success of the advert was demonstrated by a 13½ per cent increase in turnover at the garden centre during the nine weeks of the promotion.

A survey was undertaken after the promotion to assess the effect of this type of advertisement on the public. 64 per cent of people questioned who had seen the advertisement agreed that it had aroused their curiosity and that it had encouraged them to visit the garden centre in question. Once the customers were in the centre, they looked around the store and, more often than not, they were persuaded to buy something.

Printed Brochure Advertising

This can be an effective form of advertising if sufficient effort is made to distribute the brochures over a wide area. Your brochure should be cleverly planned to attract readers' attention and make them curious about the benefits your promotion has to offer. Describe the prize being offered as this is an incentive for people to take part. All details of how to enter and play the promotional game should be given clearly and precisely so that everyone knows what they have to do to win. State the closing date of the competition, and the date, time and place of any draw for the winner.

As well as distributing brochures, leaflets, or pamphlets to households in the area, you can hand them out to members of the public in a busy shopping precinct on a Saturday morning. But don't forget to ask permission from the owners of the site first! (The site manager will tell you who they are.)

If you don't have a large family to distribute brochures for you, use the services of a professional agency or contact your local youth club. They may agree to distribute them in return for a donation to their funds.

Put leaflets on display in your store and place one inside the wrapping of every item purchased. Ask other shopkeepers to distribute leaflets on your behalf. Think about your clientele and find ways to get literature to them. For example, if your shop attracts male customers, ask the local barber if he will take some of your leaflets. The men can read them while waiting for attention! In return for this service, you could offer to advertise the barber's shop on your premises. This reciprocal way of working will benefit both parties.

Advertising In Local Free Advertising Newspapers

Free advertising newspapers have become very popular recently. They are widely distributed and widely read in the area they serve, and the cost of advertising in them is less than it is in other papers. Don't forget to use some form of gimmick to draw attention to the advertisement, and use one of the ploys already described to encourage people to take part in your promotional scheme.

Advertising In Magazines

There are probably many specialist magazines that advertise and promote directly or indirectly the type of product that you have for sale. A marketing organisation will advise you which are the best ones to use for advertising your product and your promotional venture. Such an organisation will also give details of charges for advertisements of different sizes in all the various magazines.

National magazines reach a wide audience, but if you are only aiming for a local market, the charges may well prove prohibitive.

Magazines and leaflets produced by local societies, charities, clubs, schools, churches, etc., are often good places to advertise. Details of local organisations can be found in your library or local Citizens' Advice Bureau.

Don't forget: It is important to design an advertisement which will attract the eye of readers. This is especially true when your advertisement is going to appear on the same page as dozens of others. A promise of a free competition or a free draw usually encourages more people to respond, so by offering something to benefit the reader, you will immediately attract more attention to your advertisement.

Advertising On A Public Address System

If you have use of a public address system, you should not be afraid to use it to tell people about your project. Advertise in this way at the busiest times of day. Make sure that details of your venture are given in a clear and lively manner.

Roof Rack Advertising

The more unusual the form of advertising, the more effective it will be in attracting the eye. One excellent way to advertise any commodity is to use your own car – and if you are lucky, use the vehicles that belong to family and friends who are willing to help!

Fit roof racks on to all the vehicles to be used, and clamp small advertising boards on to them (see Figure 2, which illustrates how this should be done). This form of advertising is so effective simply because people don't expect to see a poster on the roof of a car and they are curious to read what it says.

A friend who owned a small car service depot advertised car tyre fitting in this way and was amazed by the response. No other form of advertising had been nearly so effective. When he questioned his customers they explained that they had not bothered to read the posters displayed inside his premises, but the same poster placed over the roof of his car had caught their attention immediately. His trade increased dramatically.

[25]

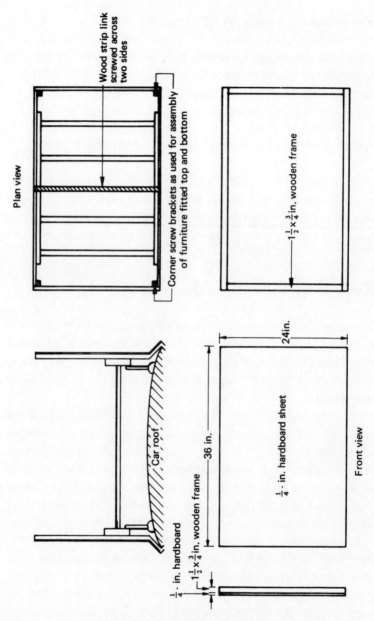

Plan view

Wood strip link screwed across two sides

Corner screw brackets as used for assembly of furniture fitted top and bottom

$1\frac{1}{2} \times \frac{3}{4}$ in. wooden frame

Car roof

$\frac{1}{4}$ - in. hardboard

$1\frac{1}{2} \times \frac{3}{4}$ in. wooden frame

$\frac{1}{4}$ - in. hardboard sheet

24 in.

36 in.

Front view

FIGURE 2.   Roof rack advertising

[26]

Charity Sponsored Walk

Sponsored walks are becoming very popular and they attract a great deal of attention. Another very effective way of advertising is to sponsor a walker to display your posters very clearly, for all to see, on a sandwich board similar to the one in Figure 3.

FIGURE 3. Sandwich board for sponsored walkers

Ask the walker to wear your board along the route, and people will automatically look at the posters on it and read what they say, both front and back. They will not be able to resist this unusual means of advertising. It is relatively cheap and very effective, especially if the walker travels down busy roads where there are crowds of people watching. Even if your poster-wearer is only one of a crowd, you will reach a wide audience and get maximum impact. Obviously, if several walkers are sponsored, the effect is enhanced.

Other Forms Of Advertising

Once your promotion is running smoothly, the best advertising medium in the world will start working for you and that is word of mouth.

But always keep looking for unusual ways in which to advertise your promotion, and remember that it is the unorthodox and unconventional that attracts most public attention.

Keep looking out for new and enterprising forms of advertising in your area. Study these outlets carefully because they may have something for you. For instance, for a small fee you might be allowed to advertise on posters at school fêtes, at local football cup matches, or at other special events that attract a large number of people.

If you are willing to spend a little more than usual on advertising your promotion, think very carefully before deciding which medium to use and which is the best way to introduce your venture to the public. Your family and friends can help you here. Ask them which form of advertising most attracts them. More important, ask them WHY, because maybe then you'll get some ideas on how to conduct your own advertising project. But do not tell your friends why you are asking the questions: they may unwittingly give you the answers they think you WANT to hear rather than what they really mean.

Consider the answers carefully in relationship to your

knowledge of all the local advertising media available, then choose the one which will be most effective for you within the constraints of your budget.

5

SOME POINTS TO CONSIDER
BEFORE STARTING

Good Planning And Organisation

Even a modest promotional scheme must be well organised and above suspicion from start to finish. You should plan every detail in advance so that things run smoothly, in a professional and responsible way. The honesty, integrity and efficiency of the operation must never be in any doubt. To feel confidence, members of the public must be able to see for themselves that the promotion is run competently and is fair to all. No amount of extra cash spent will make up for bad organisation and administration.

Small firms can achieve excellent results by using the competitions described in this book, but care must be taken to follow all the instructions given. You cannot afford to take short cuts and run the risk of causing problems that may lead on to chaos.

Remember, don't try to organise a promotional venture unless you are prepared to plan and administer the operation in a legal, fair and professional manner. Every aspect of the promotion must be clearly understood by those who are operating it, as well as by members of the public. There should be nothing left

[30]

to chance. Do not leave yourself open to complaint, however unjustified, about mismanagement, unfair dealings or fraud. It is not enough to know yourself that you are offering your public a fair deal; you have to convince them too.

Budget Carefully

You must decide at the outset how much money you want to spend on the promotion. This figure will have to include the cost of advertising, printing, administration and prizes.

Before embarking on a promotion, study the amount of business increase you need to pay for the cost of the promotion and make a reasonable profit. In this way you will have a target to aim for. You should not overspend, but at the same time nor should you try to run things on a shoestring. A cheap, penny-pinching operation can look unattractive and amateurish to members of the public, who will not support the scheme unless they are convinced of its integrity and viability.

None of the promotions in this book are expensive to operate, but you must still make every effort to work within your planned financial limitations and keep your target in mind. There is no point in spending money on a promotion if it cannot create the anticipated increase in turnover to make you a handsome profit; breaking even is not good enough.

There is no greater handicap to success than having to waste energy worrying about financial loss if the promotion does not reach its expected target. You should never rely on a promotional venture to bring in money to pay debts. Pressures like these can lead to all sorts of errors of judgement. Success comes with peace of mind and confidence, and when you have had time to think matters through in a calm and sensible way.

I give these warnings not because I think promotions might fail but because some people tend to splash out unnecessarily. They sometimes have quite unrealistic ideas about what profit they can expect to achieve from a modest promotion. Remember that a massive outlay does NOT automatically ensure the massive increase in turnover required to meet the higher cost involved.

So, make sure that your company can take in its stride the expense of whatever promotional venture you choose: in that way, if it does not bring an increase in profits straight away, you will not be in immediate difficulty. If you have any doubt about your ability to meet anticipated costs without a serious drain on capital reserves, choose a promotion that is less costly to run. You could find it just as effective.

Can You Cope With The Extra Work?

A successful promotion will obviously increase turnover to an appreciable extent, yet this factor is not always taken into account when people start a promotional campaign. It is important. There is no point in embarking on a promotion that increases the number of sales or repairs, say, if you have neither the time, the equipment, the space nor the staff needed to cope with the extra demand. Failure at this point, with resulting loss of good will, can do your firm irreparable harm, to the point where it might have been better not to have bothered with the promotion in the first place.

This may sound obvious, but the problem is not so easy to avoid as you might think. At one time the British car industry lost a very large percentage of its business to overseas competitors because it could not meet demand after a very successful promotional venture. There was a six-month delivery delay on British cars, whereas foreign ones were immediately available from stock. Understandably, customers opted to buy foreign cars instead. And the situation was made even worse for British cars when customers discovered how good the foreign ones were and how promptly they could obtain service and parts for them!

They may never have known this had British cars been available. So, British industry lost out.

Remember the old saying, 'Customers want their goods yesterday and not tomorrow.' It is still true. People do not like waiting and if delays are prolonged, they may look elsewhere.

Choosing The Right Promotion

To attract business away from rivals, you need to know which items in your shop are most affected by competition from local firms. You may need to do some research into why a previously popular item is not selling so well all of a sudden. Find out which retailers are supplying your ex-customers and discover what service it is that is luring people away from your shop. Then learn from these findings.

Choose a promotion from this book that will best counteract the problem. Your choice will, to some extent, depend on the item you are going to promote and the type of customer you are hoping to attract. You must take into account the age and sex of your customers. Discover their likes and dislikes and, if possible, make use of modern trends of the day. In the end, though, it is down to you. You are the only one who knows your clientele. Just find the promotion to suit them and you're bound to succeed.

A good promotional venture is one that is enjoyable for everyone, not only the customer but also those who operate it. If the promotion offers challenge, entertainment and fun, it will arouse the interest and imagination of everyone. The more popular and stimulating the promotion, the greater will be both your long-term and short-term success.

Know The Abilities Of Your Staff

Efficiency is the key to success. Never embark on a promotional venture until you are fully satisfied that you and your staff can administer the project efficiently to a satisfactory conclusion. No one knows the strength and weaknesses of your staff better than

[33]

you do, so use this knowledge. Choose a promotion which really suits those who are to be most involved with it.

All the operators, both you and your staff, must understand the mechanism of the promotional idea in every minute detail. Good communication is vital. Don't start the promotion until people are fully conversant with the role they have to play and feel confident that they can perform their tasks in a professional manner.

Where possible, delegate responsibility. People like to feel important and to know that you are relying on them. They will succeed in the role you have given them if you help them to take a pride in what they are doing and if you have made clear the reason for their involvement.

If you've chosen a promotion that is well within the capabilities of everyone concerned, one to suit your business and to suit the ability and personalities of your staff, the venture is certain to prove a success.

Engage The Support Of Your Staff

Any promotional activity is only as good as the people running it. Encourage your staff to develop their interest in the idea, because you must be certain of their enthusiasm and their willingness to promote the competition if the project is to work. They are the ones who MUST fire members of the public with enthusiasm for the promotion. They should explain the benefits to be derived and encourage customer participation. If staff members are not enthusiastic, they will infect customers with their apathy and lack of interest, and the promotion will not be a success.

As has been pointed out, it is always wise to take time and trouble in planning a promotional event. Attention to detail is vital if the operation is to run smoothly and well, and this planning must be done in co-operation with the people who are involved – your staff. If you ignore them and take them for granted, they may be resentful. By telling them what results you are hoping to achieve, how they and the company will benefit from increased turnover, and by asking for and using their ideas, you will involve them in the promotion and they wil' do their best to see that it works well.

The desire to succeed is essential, and once you are all pulling together, you cannot fail.

Be Sure That You Can Sustain The Promotion For The Length Of Time Required

Most good promotional schemes need to be sustained for a period of approximately seven or eight weeks. It is important to determine in advance just how long the promotion is going to run, so that you can pace yourself and take steps to ensure that it continues to flourish for the full length of time.

The first SEVEN days of the promotion are vital, for it is during this time that most of the hard work is done – advertising the promotion, letting people know how it works and telling them about the benefits that they can derive by participating. You must make a great effort to ensure that you get this information across to your public in the first few days of the promotion.

As explained, it is not always appreciated that the success of the promotion will depend on the hard work, enthusiasm and support of those who are administering it. Make sure that the staff have the necessary determination to see the project through to its conclusion.

There may well be extra work for everyone during the period of a promotion, so make sure that your staff have time to complete the tasks they are given. Every possible encouragement and help should be given to ensure that the extra effort needed during the period of the promotion is sustained not just for the first day or two but for the duration of the campaign.

Offer High Standards

When organising any promotional activity, always ensure that the goods on display are clean and attractive to the eye and make sure that they are displayed in a pleasing manner. To be attractive and to impress your customers, displays should be neither too cluttered nor too sparse. Window dressing is an art and it pays to take the time and the trouble to make the shop window and also the counter displays a pleasure to behold.

Application forms, leaflets, advertising propaganda and other printed matter should be of an acceptably high standard. Poor printing on low-quality paper can adversely affect people psychologically, giving the unfortunate impression that the promotion is operated by amateurs on a very limited budget. People might then be disinclined to take an interest and might even wonder about the viability and integrity of the promotion. That is obviously not the reaction you want.

This does not imply that an exorbitant amount of money should be spent on the accessories for the promotion to be a success. If you shop around you will find materials of an acceptable standard that will not overstretch your budget and yet will give your promotion that special uplift that it deserves.

It pays to spend a little extra on advertising in newspapers. Short, sparse advertisements which are scantily worded and which omit important details do not inspire readers. Take a special interest in the wording and design of posters and newspaper advertisements and the results will justify the expenditure of money and effort.

Avoid Conflict With Suppliers

A promotion scheme can sometimes cause unexpected conflict with suppliers, and this is counter-productive. Be aware of the problem and take precautions so that you don't fall into the trap!

If, for example, as part of your promotion you offer discount on foreign tyres which are the same quality as, or perhaps even better than, the tyres you buy from other regular suppliers, then your normal suppliers are bound to feel upset. In the long term this can cause problems, because although you might make a profit by selling a large consignment of cheap foreign tyres, the success of the promotion will be very short-lived if your regular suppliers retaliate in some way for their loss of trade! They may refuse to sell you other important items that you need and cannot easily obtain elsewhere. If this were to happen, the consequences would obviously be detrimental to your business and all the benefits of the promotion could be destroyed.

To avoid this problem, discuss any plans for a forthcoming promotion with your various agents. If they have reservations, they will tell you, and hopefully you will be able to reach some form of compromise acceptable to both parties at this stage.

If you cannot agree on the product that you want to promote, you need to weigh up the profit you hope to achieve against any losses that you might incur by upsetting regular suppliers who would have preferred you to promote one of their products!

Find What Support You Can Get From Suppliers

Most product suppliers admire people who engage in private enterprise, and if a promotion encourages the sales of their product to rise, they are even more appreciative! It is a good idea to approach the area representatives of your various suppliers and tell them about your plans to undertake a promotional venture. Most representatives will be keen to approach their employers in an endeavour to enlist their support. Remember, they receive a commission on the sale of goods, so it is money in their pockets if your promotion is successful and the sale of their products increases.

You could offer to make one of the supplier's products a leader in the campaign in exchange for the manufacturer's support. Do not be discouraged by one or two refusals. As the saying goes: 'If you don't ask, you can't receive'. Just use a refusal to bait another supplier who sells the same type of goods!

When consulting suppliers, it is helpful if you can give them written details of any research you have undertaken prior to the promotion. The paperwork will explain *why* you think the item you have chosen to promote has the most appeal in your area. These written details will impress the sales director, whom the representative will be approaching, and you will have more chance of winning support.

Suppliers could obviously help in a number of ways. They could offer goods at special discount, to lure you away from cut-price rivals, or they could agree to pay the cost of advertising and/or the printing of stationery, posters, application forms, etc. Alternatively, they could offer a cash prize or a prize in the form of goods. The amount and type of help given by various suppliers will obviously depend on a number of factors, but it is always worth trying to enlist their support.

Offer A Suitable Prize

When deciding on a prize, you must always have in mind the type of person you will be attracting by your promotion. This may sound obvious, but it is surprising how often people make this mistake. For example, one fund-raising group offered a prize of 'a full course of driving lessons' in a community where most people could not afford to tax and run a car. The organisers had not taken this fact into account when they launched the competition and were naturally disappointed at the poor public response. Likewise, there would be no point in offering an exciting adventure holiday for children in an area inhabited mainly by retired people. Few would be interested in such a prize.

A good prize is one that will provoke great public interest and give a lot of pleasure and enjoyment to the winner. It is human nature to want to win something for nothing, and the offer of a worthwhile prize stimulates the competitive instinct. If people really want to win the prize, they will have no alternative but to enter the competition, and all at once your promotion is off the ground to a good start.

Select The Time Of Year Most Suitable For Your Promotion

The timing of a promotional venture can be very important so before deciding when to launch the project, take the following factors into consideration:

1. October and November are good months for many types of promotion, especially those that offer discount or reduction on the price of goods that are suitable for Christmas presents.

2. March and April are also good months for launching a promotional campaign, because these are the months when people are buying goods in preparation for their summer vacations.

3. Promotional activity is best ignored during the holiday months of June, July and August unless you operate in a holiday resort, in which case you should take advantage of the holiday season and run a promotion at this time to attract more trade.

4. Never launch a campaign immediately after Christmas or during the January sales, when people are jaded and not in the mood for any kind of promotional activity.

Make Sure That The Promotion Is Conducted In A Fair And Legal Way

As has been explained, it is important that all competitions you organise for your promotional venture are run fairly. More than that. They must be seen to be run in an honest and professional way if you wish to avoid accusations of unfairness, mismanagement, cheating, fraud or deceit.

Make sure that rules and regulations are clearly written on application forms and displayed in the shop. Advertise the day, time and place of a public draw or other event. Do everything possible to ensure that every entry to a competition has an equal chance of winning the prize. A competition that is open to members of the public must be carefully supervised to ensure that there are no loopholes for those who might try to cheat.

Draws must be made in a public place where they can be seen to be operating legally and within the law. If a winning ticket is to be drawn, ask a member of the public to do it. The person who draws the winning ticket must be someone who has not entered the competition and who therefore cannot win the prize.

If there are doubts or queries as to whether a competition, or the procedure for running a competition, is legal or not, ask members of the Gaming and Lotteries Board or look for answers in the Gaming and Lotteries Acts, although these are very complicated. Having said that, none of the promotions outlined in this book will contravene the Gaming and Lotteries Acts if they are operated as directed. Remember, though, that these acts CAN be unwittingly abused, and if there is even the slightest doubt of the legality of a scheme, then never be afraid to make enquiries before you proceed with a new and different form of promotion.

Take Action To Maintain Your Increased Trade

Organisers of promotional schemes should aim for an increase in turnover of at least 20 per cent. If the promotion is really successful, it should give an increase in turnover of 30 per cent or more.

If returns show that this figure is not being met, and it seems likely that it won't be, then you must look quickly and carefully into what has gone wrong. Check each aspect of the operation to find out where it is falling down, and then rectify the situation immediately, before it is too late. It is always possible to rescue a failing promotion and get it on to a firmer footing, provided you take the right action.

Every promotion you start should incorporate additional plans to maintain and increase the extra business that you gain during the promotion. Short-term gains can be detrimental to your business rather than beneficial. Once you have attracted new customers, you must maintain and develop the service you offer. Never allow a steady decline in trade. With just a little effort on your part, any downward trend can be reversed and your firm can enjoy continuous success.

Part 3

CASE HISTORIES

6

THE PETROL STATION

The following is the story of one man's experience of how serious competition can be overcome.

Back in 1951 my work took me to Belfast, and I decided to pay my Uncle Jack a surprise visit. He was a lively person, full of fun, and totally devoted to running his own garage and petrol station. He had invested all his money in the purchase of the business many years before, and thanks to his dedication, perseverance and hard work, he had developed it into a flourishing concern. He loved cars and took great pride in servicing, maintaining and repairing them for his customers, as well as supplying petrol and spare parts.

Uncle Jack had reason to be proud of his achievements. He had built up his firm from strength to strength and his reputation for providing good value for money was widespread. He was a first-class mechanic and he employed reliable staff who could meet his customers' demands quickly, efficiently and well. Thanks to all this, he was able to enjoy a high standard of living, better than he could ever have envisaged when he first purchased the dilapidated garage premises many years before. So, he was a hard-working man, proud of his relationship with loyal customers and financially very secure.

I expected to be greeted by his usual warm, sunny smile, but as soon as I saw him I knew that something was terribly wrong. He was sitting slumped in his chair in a very dejected manner, as if his world had just come to an end. Usually such a forceful character, he now seemed locked in a state of almost morbid depression. He was wrapped in a shroud of self-pity and despair.

When I asked Jack what was wrong, he replied that his life had been shattered. He was falling into debt and could see no way to recover his losses. He was a beaten man. Yet when I had last visited him, a few months before, he had described all his various business activities and future plans in his usual confident and enthusiastic manner. There had been no hint that his livelihood would soon be threatened or that his dreams would suddenly be dashed. He had never previously entertained such pessimistic thoughts.

I poured him a stiff drink and made him tell his story. Apparently a national motor service station had opened a new branch nearby, just 200 yards from his own empire, and Jack was losing all his customers. With flashy promotions, cut-price petrol and all sorts of hard to resist 'special offers', the new firm was attracting a great deal of local support. It seemed to have unlimited resources at its disposal and had just completed an intensive publicity campaign and some clever promotional tactics to lure away most of Jack's regular customers. As a result, it was enjoying great prosperity, while Uncle Jack's turnover had been drastically reduced and his margin of profit had slumped.

Jack felt demoralised because his rival's workshop was equipped with all the latest gadgets and machinery. He knew he could never survive simply by cutting the price of his petrol. The new company management had powers to undercut his prices however much these were reduced. He didn't know what to do. After years of hard work and sacrifice he was suddenly faced with the type of competition that he felt totally unable to deal with: 'I am very small fry in comparison to a national concern like that,' he complained. 'How can I compete with a firm that has the backing of high finance and unlimited resources? My future is over!'

I was very disheartened to hear this story. How sad it was that a man's livelihood could be threatened in this way! He had convinced himself that he faced bankruptcy and a ruined career. What made things worse for him was that he felt betrayed. He had enjoyed regular support from customers on whom he felt he could depend because they had been using his garage facilities for many years. But now that the newcomer had arrived they had been lured away by the offer of special attractions that he could not provide. 'I don't blame them, of course,' he said disconsolately, 'but this predicament has hurt my pride as well as my pocket. I tell you, I am a broken man.'

I had heard similar heartbreaking stories many times, but somehow I had never expected Jack to succumb to such a defeatist attitude. He was ready to quit before the fight had begun. By giving way to his feelings of inadequacy he had blocked any capacity for positive thought and action.

I have always believed that we can find a solution to every problem if only we take the trouble to think constructively, but Jack was never going to make progress by filling his mind with thoughts of doom and gloom. I refused to accept that his dilemma was without a solution, for large multinationals have their problems too – and this can be to the advantage of the smaller well-run organisation.

Large, multinational companies with many branches and subsidiary companies inevitably suffer complex and cumbersome administration, communication and management procedures. Any new policy or innovation being considered by a local area office has to go through a series of different committees before the go-ahead is given. Even then, it is the duty of the head office to make decisions about what the local area office staff must do to keep within the law. The set of procedures and rules must be uniform in all branches. A new venture can take a very long time to put into operation, with various committee members arguing

)ating each aspect of the project! When the plan of action is finally agreed upon, organisation and administration can be cumbersome and slow.

For these reasons, employees of large firms tend not to make the effort to try to improve and upgrade local services. They conform to management rules because this keeps them out of trouble and is less work for them in the long run. Red tape and company rules are an effective deterrent to progress at times.

Knowledge of this state of affairs is good news for the small business. Uncle Jack, for instance, was not restricted by ponderous and complex management problems. He did not have to keep within the rules of a vast empire, nor did he have a lot of other area managers to please. He was his own boss and was therefore in a position to make his own decisions. He could think of an idea one morning and be acting on it by the afternoon if he wanted to. This was where he had a big advantage over his competitors.

Naturally, I reminded Jack of the problems faced by large companies and I assured him that there must be a commodity that he could sell or a service that he could provide which his rival could not offer local people – at least, not for a very long time to come!

At first he refused to be placated in this way. He could think of nothing that he could afford to provide which would disadvantage his competitors. I could not believe this, so we debated the issue well into the night, until I suddenly came up with an answer: a Motorists' Club! Uncle Jack knew his profession well, he knew many of the firms in his area and also many of the people who lived locally. He wanted to provide a service that would satisfy the needs of the community and a Motorists' Club seemed the obvious answer.

I started to explain my idea. 'If you plan the operation of the club carefully, you can offer facilities that your competitor can never supply. You can also offer special discounts without affecting your budget too badly.' I listed the advantages that motorists would derive from joining:

1. Discount on petrol.

2. Discounts on repairs.

3. Discounts on accessories purchased in the shop.

4. Discounts on new cars.

5. Discounts from other retail outlets – even from retail outlets not connected with the motor trade. He could persuade shops and other firms to offer discounts to his customers who produced their membership cards. This would be his trump card and a major attraction.

In return for these benefits, members of the public would be asked to pay a fee to join the club and an annual subscription thereafter. If there were sufficient people paying, he could easily afford the discounts that he offered.

Jack began to feel excited by the idea: 'If people join my club, they will remain loyal to me because they have paid their subscription and they will want value for their money,' he said happily.

I was pleased. At last he was beginning to think more positively and I could see that he was getting his fighting spirit back. I was sure that the idea was good. Jack's club members could save a lot of money by purchasing goods offered at discount prices. The wider the selection of retail outlets that participated in the scheme, the greater would be the advantage of club membership. The membership fee would be a small price to pay for the advantages to be enjoyed.

Manufacturers and retail outlets would benefit greatly by offering a discount to the club members. Firms that operated within a radius of twenty-five miles would surely agree to participate because Jack would be putting a great deal of extra trade their way, and they would be given the advantage of the free publicity. Their increase in profit should cover the cost of a small discount on each order.

We discussed the plan at length. I advised Jack to contact a number of local firms to obtain their initial reaction to the idea of offering his club members special discount. If local firms were interested, he could have a number of application forms for club membership printed. These forms, giving details of the project, would be distributed to as many households as possible.

Jack was thrilled with the idea and felt sure it would work. Even his competitor up the road could not offer a service like this. Such organisation would be quite outside their normal scope of operation. Even if they did try to launch a similar service locally, by the time they were ready to start, Jack's scheme would be already well established and his club members would have no need to join a second, similar scheme.

Jack's excitement was a tonic for me. He was looking forward to starting work on his new campaign already. After all, he had nothing to lose and everything to gain! He was already rising to the challenge. 'It is too late tonight, but tomorrow I will start making my enquiries,' he promised.

When I left, he was looking forward to the following day, not facing each hour with a deeper and deeper feeling of inadequacy and depression. I felt confident that the Motorists' Club would work, and now he had a reason to agree with me and could face the future with hope and determination.

Within the next few days Jack had received positive answers from his regular customers. They liked the idea of joining his Motorists' Club. He had also received firm offers of participation from both small and very large firms. After all, he was offering them a guarantee of more custom and extra income without any effort on their part. And for the price of their discount he was giving them extra publicity as well. No wonder they were glad to co-operate!

As soon as he had received written confirmation of agreements to provide discounts for his members from a sufficient number of firms, he had 25,000 leaflets printed and distributed around the homes in his area. In return for a fee to boost their funds, the local scouts agreed to make the deliveries on his behalf.

Within a few weeks Uncle Jack had obtained 1,754 fully paid-up members. Each person, having paid their fee, was in fact paying to become his customer! In twelve months he had trebled his membership, and he never looked back again. In spite of the severe competition that had frightened him so much at first, he was able to develop and maintain a very prosperous business. He even had to build an extension to his premises and employ more staff to meet growing demand.

The club flourished for eighteen years, until Jack was forced to retire for health reasons, and at the time he retired he was issuing a printed booklet to his customers which listed over 100 firms that offered special discounts to all those who produced his membership cards.

See Promotion 1 for further details on how to organise a Motorists' Club.

7

THE PUBLIC HOUSE

I hope you have taken heart after reading the last chapter! The motto is THINK POSITIVE when faced with increasing competition and a consequent fall in business turnover. Never let your mind become blocked with thoughts of defeat. It is usually possible to find a way to meet the challenge of competition, and Uncle Jack is only one of tens of thousands of people who have proved this.

We were lucky on that occasion to be able to think of an idea so quickly, but sometimes the solution is not immediately apparent. If this is the case, try talking your problem over with regular customers. They will often be able to make suggestions and give good advice on the best way to improve the service you offer.

I once suggested this to the owner of a pub in the West Midlands who was anxious to improve his trade. He was astonished at the idea of involving his clients, and replied jokingly: 'I am quite frightened at the prospect of the replies I will get to my question of what changes people would like to see made in my pub!'

Nevertheless, he agreed to my plan and was most pleasantly surprised to find that his customers really enjoyed conversing with him in this way. It made them feel important and they wanted to be involved in any new innovations that would affect them.

I suggested one or two attractions that might bring in the extra custom that he required. He discussed these ideas at length with his regulars, who became quite excited at the proposed changes. New ideas were thought of and plans were made as to how they could be put into effect for the benefit of all concerned.

The attitude of local people was very positive. They were determined to see the new schemes working successfully in their pub. But if the landlord had simply presented the innovations to them as a *fait accompli*, they would never have become so involved. Results were better than the landlord had ever expected, because his clients worked just as hard as he did to put my ideas into operation.

The following were some of the schemes used to attract people back to that old pub:

1. Improvements were made in the seating arrangements: people were given more space and no sitting or standing was allowed at the bar.

2. A promotional competition was launched, and the publican and his staff made an enthusiastic and determined effort to draw it to their customers' attention. In the past they had made very little effort on this front, depending on the publicity printed on the back of beer mats to advertise and promote their wares, and their apathy had infected the regulars.

My friend was amazed at how well people responded to an enthusiastic and personal approach. People liked having the promotion explained to them and they were perfectly willing to participate once their interest had been aroused.

3. A series of pub 'Fun Nights' were organised. On these evenings the publican made a party atmosphere by planning and organising games and competitions for people to play. This was a great success, as the party atmosphere enabled people to mix freely and enjoy the novelty and the fun. Attendance on these nights was always good.

[53]

4. A 'Pub Regulars' Club' was started. This proved to be very popular, encouraging local people to drink here rather than anywhere else because of the benefits they received. Members were given a card with thirty-five blank spaces. Each time they purchased a drink, or a round of drinks, they had their card stamped by bar staff. When all the spaces were stamped, the holders of the cards were entitled to a discount of 5p on all their own drinks for the rest of the year.

My friend found that his enthusiasm and determination to improve conditions in his pub inspired his customers, and they in turn were keen to see the improvements working effectively for the benefit of the community. Local people encouraged their friends and relatives to drink at the pub and the atmosphere became one of friendly companionship. Everyone was proud of their part in the achievements and the pub grew from strength to strength.

See Promotions 13, 31, 32, 33, 34 and 35 in particular for ways of increasing interest in your pub.

Part 4

THE PROMOTIONS

1. The Motorists' Discount Club

This car club venture operates very effectively, and it enables owners of small, privately owned garages to compete successfully with their larger competitors. The service provided is very popular with members of the public and is easy to run, yet the area depots of large national firms tend to find it impossible to handle the sort of administration involved.

Equipment needed

- Leaflets/application forms (see Figure 4).
- Membership cards.
- Notebook for record-keeping.

The promotion

Car owners are invited to pay £5 to join a Motorists' Discount Club. Thereafter they pay an annual subscription of £5 in return for the following benefits:

1. Discount on petrol, car servicing, car sales, motor parts and all motoring accessories sold by the operator.

2. Discount on a wide variety of goods and services provided by local firms within a radius of approximately five miles.

Firms you might like to approach to give discount to club members could usefully include travel agents, caravan suppliers, new and second-hand car dealers, freezer food suppliers, insurance brokers and motoring organisations. Try to negotiate with one supplier of every type of commodity that might be useful to motorists.

Remember that you must NOT do trade with any two companies that offer the same facilities because the managements of the companies involved must be satisfied that your club members will buy only from them when they wish to purchase cut-price goods or services. If they are the sole supplier on your list and are offering specially low rates, they want to be guaranteed the exclusive custom of your members.

Manufacturers, as well as wholesalers and retailers, will be happy to participate in the scheme since you will be including the name of their company on your list, which means free advertising. The discount that these firms offer should be well compensated for by the good publicity and extra custom that they receive in return.

It is anticipated that the cost of organising and administering the launch of the Motorists' Club will be met from subscription fees.

Have printed a minimum of 1,000 leaflets describing the service provided. These will also serve as membership application forms.

The printed leaflets can be delivered to households within a five-mile radius of the garage. You may be able to persuade a youth organisation to undertake this task in return for a donation to their cause.

The forms can also be distributed to people in car parks within a twenty-mile radius of the garage. Don't be tempted to leave advertising propaganda on the windscreens of cars: this practice is illegal and you will leave yourself open to prosecution.

Let local firms know about the club. You could visit the management and give them a copy of your leaflet to pin up on the noticeboard so that all their employees have an opportunity to join.

Before accepting hundreds of new members into the club, it is important to decide in advance how many members, and how much extra work, your firm can handle in comfort and without undue strain. It is ESSENTIAL that club membership be kept within manageable bounds. It would be disastrous to find yourself not equipped to meet all the demands that new members can make.

When people join the club, they are paying for a service which you are legally bound to provide. If you cannot honour your obligations, you could find yourself being reported to the Office of Fair Trading, and this could bring your good name into disrepute. The law will not accept as an excuse the fact that you underestimated the demands that would be made upon you when you launched the club. So, plan carefully, taking into account the size of your existing premises, the number of staff and the provision of machines and equipment. Remember that with a sudden influx of members you may find yourself inundated with requests for car servicing and repairs. And you MUST be in a position to maintain your usual high standards of workmanship because long delays before work can be done will mean that people soon become disillusioned with the club and you will lose your good will.

So, remember, before you launch the club, decide how many members you can comfortably serve and restrict membership to that number.

Each membership card should have the owner's photograph (passport-size) attached, because membership cards must not be shared with non-members. It may help to allocate everyone their own membership number as this serves to identify members and will be useful for your records.

Do you want to save money and cut down the cost of repairs to your car?

THEN JOIN OUR MOTORISTS' CLUB.

Question HOW CAN THE MOTORISTS' CLUB HELP YOU TO SAVE?

Answer IN MANY WAYS.

1. We are offering a 10 per cent discount on all car servicing.

2. We are offering a 10 per cent discount on the price of all accessories and parts that you buy from our shop.

3. We have secured the offer of discount from suppliers of many goods and services for all our members who produce their membership cards. Members can benefit from a reduction in price on all of the following goods and services: new car sales, tyres, caravan sales, ferry travel, holidays in the UK and abroad, reduced fees to join a motoring organisation, theatre and nightclub tickets, restaurant meals, hotel accommodation and travel by coach.

4. We are currently negotiating to obtain discount on other items that our members have requested. These include discount from local firms that sell jewellery, clothing and fashion accessories, leather goods, electrical equipment, children's toys, books, etc.

Just think about it

The discount offered on only one or two items could reimburse your annual subscription to the club. From then onwards you are in profit.

How do you join?

Just complete the coupon attached and return it to THE MOTORISTS' DISCOUNT CLUB, PADDY'S AUTO SERVICE AND REPAIRS, Main Road, Poppyton, Cornwall, together with £10, which includes £5 membership fee and £5 annual subscription for club membership.

THE MOTORISTS' DISCOUNT CLUB

Please enclose a passport photograph which can be attached to your membership card.

The Motorists' Discount Club is the only local club of its kind, and so we are offering cut-price reductions that only our members can share and enjoy. Regretfully we are compelled to limit the number of members we can accept, so join early if you want to avoid disappointment. We are looking forward to meeting you and we hope soon to accept you as a member of this exclusive club.

- -

I WISH TO JOIN THE MOTORISTS' DISCOUNT CLUB.

Name...
(Block capitals)

Address..

....

Telephone...

I enclose a cheque/postal order for £10 to include the enrolment fee of £5 and the annual subscription of £5.
   I also enclose a passport photograph for use on my membership card.

Member's signature...

Date of application..

FIGURE 4. Sample leaflet/application form

2. Build A Slogan

This competition is suitable for any retail outlet which supplies goods to regular local customers. Because it boosts the sales of the goods it's promoting, you should be able to enlist the support of the manufacturer or supplier.

Never be afraid to ask your suppliers to help in some way with the promotion. They may donate a worthwhile prize, pay for printing or give some other form of assistance. After all, it's their product you're trying to sell, and they will benefit as much as you do if the promotion is a success.

Equipment needed

- Approximately 10,000 slips of paper, 1 in. × ½ in.

- Descriptive words relevant to the product written, typed or printed on each slip of paper.

- Entry forms on which the slips of paper must be fixed in word order to form a sentence (see Figure 5).

- A drum.

The promotion

Choose the product that you wish to promote and the three people who are going to be your panel of judges.

When customers buy goods, they are given a receipt and a slip of paper on which a word is printed. Customers save receipts and slips until they have enough descriptive words to form a humorous and original sentence. The slogan should comprise at least nine words and describe the product, or the effect the product has on the user!

When choosing the words to type or print on the slips of paper, you must select ones that are stimulating, vital and relevant to the product in question. Remember that in order

BUILD A SLOGAN

Each time you are given a receipt for goods purchased at this store, you will be invited to draw a slip from a drum on the counter.

On each slip is written a word which is to be used in the construction of a witty sentence to describe '. . . . . . BARS' and to say why they appeal to you.

YOUR SLOGAN MUST HAVE A MINIMUM OF NINE WORDS

TWO SLOGANS ONLY ARE ACCEPTED FROM EACH CUSTOMER.

Only use words that have been drawn from the drum and for which you have been given a receipt. When you have collected sufficient words to compose a witty sentence, stick the slips on to the entry form in correct word order and write out the sentence in ink in capital letters in the space provided.

Please save your receipts as proof of purchase, and submit one receipt for each word slip in your sentence with the entry form.

A panel of three judges will examine entries to find the most apt and original slogan. Prizes will be awarded to the winner and five runners-up.

The decision of the judges will be final and binding and no correspondence will be entered into regarding the competition.

Last date of entry..

Print your first slogan here..

....

Print your second slogan here..

....

FIGURE 5. Sample entry form

[63]

Name...
(Block capitals)

Address..

....

Telephone..

Date.................................

Usual signature......................................

Affix your word slips in correct order to make a sentence here

Slogan No. I

Slogan No. II

FIGURE 5. Sample entry form

[64]

to maintain interest in the competition, you must ensure that there are enough descriptive and link words to compose imaginative sentences. If you make sure that there are only a limited number of certain words, customers will have to accumulate lots of slips if they are to make a witty sentence.

Customers are limited to ONE entry form, on which they must enter two slogans. When they have enough words, they must fix their slips of paper in word order on to the entry form and write the sentences out in full. The completed entry form must be returned to the organiser, together with one receipt for each word slip in the message, on or before the closing date advertised.

The competition should be run for a period of six weeks at the most.

The winning entry is the one that appeals most to the panel of judges, whose decision must be final and binding.

3. Match Your Purchases

Equipment needed

- A large drum.

- 4,000 or more slips of paper approximately 2 in. × 1 in., on which are printed the name of two products sold in the store. At least 30 per cent of the names should be of goods in great demand, but the majority should not. Always combine a product of low cost with a product of high cost (see Figure 6).

- A supply of shopping vouchers for £3 and £5.

- A plastic sweet jar or other container which has a slit in the lid.

The promotion

As customers bring their basket of goods to the check-out counter, they are invited to take a slip of paper from a drum. The drum should be so constructed that people can only just get their hand into the box. They must NOT be able to see the wording on the slip of paper they withdraw until they have removed their hands from the drum. If they draw out a slip which shows two of the products included in their basket, they win a shopping voucher for £3 which is redeemable in the shop.

If only one of the goods on the slip of paper is included in the basket, the customer wins nothing.

Whether customers win a prize or not, they should write their name and address on the back of the slip. This slip is then placed immediately into the plastic jar for entry in a weekly draw. At the advertised time, day and place, a customer is selected at random and asked to draw a slip from the jar in public. The person whose name appears on the back of the slip wins a shopping voucher for £5 which is redeemable at the shop.

By operating this second competition, you can ensure that the slips are not reused. It is also a useful means of checking, at the end of each business day, which slips have been drawn. These can be replaced with new slips.

Financial support of £50 from each of your major suppliers would enable you to offer good prizes for quite a considerable time.

STORK MARGARINE/BIRDS EYE COD FILLETS

---

or

ANCHOR BUTTER/BOLD WASHING POWDER

FIGURE 6. Sample promotion slips

4. Playing Card Bonanza

This promotion is very easy to operate and can be organised by pubs and various social clubs as well as by shops and other retail outlets. The competition is cheap and takes very little extra effort on the part of the staff.

Equipment needed

- A painted jar or other opaque container.
- A pack of playing cards.
- Lined paper.
- A drum or box.

The promotion

Each time customers purchase goods, they write down on the back of their receipt their name, address, telephone number and their guess as to the order in which three playing cards will be drawn from a jar at the end of the week. They then put their receipt into the drum provided.

Three cards will be drawn from the jar by a customer selected at random at the same time every Saturday until the promotion ends.

To make administration easier, the details on the receipts should be recorded on lined paper at the end of each working day. You will then be able to determine the winner at the end of the week without having to look at each entry.

People enjoy the free entry to this game, they find it fun to play, and they look forward to finding out if their guesses were correct at the end of the week.

The name of the winner and the order of cards drawn each week should be displayed after each draw. This not only

[67]

conforms to the law but also reminds people to try again for the following week.

A record of each sequence of cards actually drawn from the drum should be kept so that customers can check their entry at a later date if necessary. This avoids any possible misunderstanding. Also keep a list of the names and addresses of the winning entries each week.

Although this game is so simple to play, there are over 2,500 combinations in which three playing cards can be drawn, so it is not easy to guess the winning sequence. The game has been known to run for several weeks. If there is no winner one week, add the prize to the following week's competition, and so on, so that the winnings accumulate.

The prize offered could be a litre bottle of whisky or other spirits, or a shopping voucher for goods purchased at the store. Always try to find a supplier who is willing to donate your prizes.

5. What's In A Name?

This promotion is suitable for retail outlets that stock groceries, though of course it could be adapted to other products. People enjoy the competition because it's fun to play and provides a challenge. It is easy to organise and requires very little effort. Costs are minimal and, if you are successful in finding firms to finance the scheme, there might be no capital outlay at all.

Equipment needed

- Entry forms (see Figure 7).

- A shop stamp to mark packages of all products used in the promotion to prevent your customers from submitting labels from goods which they have purchased elsewhere.

The promotion

When customers buy goods from the shop, they are invited to cut out words from the labels of at least SIX different products. The words, or part words, must be used to form a clever and witty advertising slogan. All the letters on the labels of bottles, jars, tins, packets or whatever are acceptable.

For example, the slogan

RICH GOLDEN CHICKEN AND BIRDS DRINK TOMATO SAUCE THE EASY
WAY ON HP

is made up from words from the labels on the following goods:

Heinz golden chicken and vegetable soup
Birds instant coffee
Cadbury's drinking chocolate
Bisto gravy granules
Heinz spaghetti
HP sauce

Completed entry forms must be accompanied by the labels used for the slogan, all displaying the shop stamp. The receipts for all the goods used must also be enclosed.

Instead of cutting out the words and sticking them on to the entry form, customers could be asked to submit the stamped labels or packets that they have used. In this case they should draw a clearly marked circle around each of the words used.

Appoint a panel of three judges to pick the winning slogan. One could be a representative who calls regularly at your shop. Another could be a popular and well-known local personality. (Try to find someone who shops in your store if possible.) Their decision will be final and binding.

It should be possible to obtain financial support from suppliers of goods on sale in the shop. If labels from their goods are used, the products will have been purchased and advertised in a unique and very effective way. It should also be possible to obtain prizes

---

WHAT'S IN A NAME

Gordon's Store, 25 High Street

Write a witty and amusing slogan and win a prize

All you have to do is collect labels from at least six products purchased in this store and, using words or part-words taken from the labels, put together a humorous slogan. It's so easy!

FIX YOUR WORDS IN HERE TO FORM THE SLOGAN

WRITE YOUR SLOGAN OUT HERE IN INK IN CAPITAL LETTERS

....

....

Send this form back to us, together with receipts and the labels you used, all showing our stamp, by the closing date......................................

Name..
(Block capitals)

Address..

....

....

Telephone...

Date..

FIGURE 7. Sample entry form

[70]

from manufacturers of some of the products. If you can secure the offer of at least one very good prize, it makes the game so much more appealing to play! Alternatively, try to persuade several firms to donate £50 towards prizes. Then you could offer a shopping voucher worth £100 and several vouchers for smaller amounts for the runners-up! One of your suppliers might be prepared to supply entry forms if you agree to put their company name at the bottom of the form. In this way you can run the promotional venture at no financial cost to yourself.

This competition is very popular because it increases turnover quite substantially, as the need to obtain words for slogans encourages people to buy extra items.

6. Guess The Contents Of Tins

This competition is especially suitable for a promotion in a grocery shop, and it is good fun for people of all ages.

Equipment needed

- Six tins, each to have its top labelled from one to six.

- A sheet of paper recording the number and contents of each tin, placed inside a sealed envelope. (The wrappings on the tins can then be removed.)

- A supply of entry forms.

- A container to hold the entry forms.

The promotion

Select SIX tins of food, some popular types, like baked beans, and some less-used products, like asparagus tips! All the tins

[71]

used must be from your current stock. Number the tins and record their contents, then remove the labels so that only the number is left showing and there is no visible clue as to the contents of any of the tins.

Put the competition tins on display on a shelf in the store and invite shoppers to examine the tins – they can pick them up to feel the weight and shake them to listen to the sounds made – and then guess their contents. They must write down their answers on the forms provided. Each completed entry form must be accompanied by a receipt for goods purchased at the store valued £2 or more.

At the end of a four-week period, a customer is invited to open the sealed envelope to reveal the sheet of paper on which all the details of the competition have been recorded.

The entry forms are drawn from a drum, in public, one at a time, and the first all-correct entry drawn wins the prize.

Just in case there is no outright winner, keep to one side the first entry form drawn with five out of six of the answers correct and the first entry with four correct. The prize can then go to the entry with the highest score if there is no all-correct answer sheet.

A shopping voucher is a suitable prize, valued at approximately £30 and redeemable at your store.

A word of caution: Always ensure that you are the ONLY person present when the tins are being numbered and recorded on the list. This prevents anyone from being tempted to give the answers to a friend. It can happen!

7. Shopper's Word Puzzle

This competition is most suited to a walk-round, self-service store. It is both easy to organise and cheap to operate, especially if you are successful in securing the support of the manufacturers or suppliers of goods being promoted. It should be possible to get the support of twenty companies, if not more, when you tell them that, to play the game, customers have to write down the names of their products on the entry form and also find those names in the competition 'crossword'. This is an excellent means of advertising, because the items are committed to memory, and you are providing a free advertisement for the manufacturer for supplier who agrees to participate in the scheme.

Urge your manufacturers and suppliers to provide prizes, or to pay for printing and publicity costs. If each firm agreed to pay £100 towards the cost of the promotion, you would be able to offer several shopping vouchers as prizes, redeemable at your store. The anticipation of winning a new shopping voucher every two or three weeks will be a big draw for customers and will boost your sales.

Equipment needed

- Posters on which are printed the names of all the goods on promotion.

- Entry forms (see Figure 8). Note that some time must be spent in devising the rectangle in which the names of products being promoted are hidden.

- The shop's stamp, to mark all labels and packets of goods in the promotion.

- Twenty products to be included in the promotion.

The promotion

Compile the entry form for this competition as shown on page 75. Follow the plan carefully, as any deviation may lead

lead to problems which could well detract from the value of the promotion.

To enter the competition, shoppers must list the names of all the products shown on a poster in the store, and these are written down in the space provided on the entry form. Customers must then try to locate the items they have listed from among the letters in the rectangle on the entry form.

When all the products have been found, shoppers fill in their name and address on the entry form and place it in the box provided, together with ten or more labels that have been stamped with the name of the shop, to prove that the goods have been purchased there.

There is no limit to the number of entries that any one person can submit, so long as each entry is accompanied by the appropriate number of stamped labels from tins and packets.

Posters advertising the promotion should be placed in prominent places in the shop. They should clearly show the names of goods to be included in the promotion, as customers will need to write these names down on the entry forms. However, not all the goods used in this promotion need be included in the rectangle of letters.

Decide in advance the length of time you wish the promotion to run for. You could have a series of competitions, each lasting two or three weeks, with a new range of products for each new promotion. So as soon as one promotion has finished, another can start. In this case you will need new entry forms and a new set of posters to advertise the different range of products to be promoted.

On the closing date, a member of the public is invited to draw entries from a drum and the winner will be the first all-correct form.

Strict operation of the rules of the competition is essential. You will need the support and co-operation of your staff to ensure that the promotion is run fairly, efficiently and well.

Instructions on how to compile the shoppers' word puzzle

Take a sheet of paper and draw a square which is divided into 20×20 small squares.

Having selected the products to be used in the promotion, print them on to the squares in the manner shown, some back to front, some diagonally and some straight across. If you are using more than ten products, try to integrate the product names with each other. When the names of all the products are listed, fill in the remaining squares with random letters.

Once you have compiled the word puzzle, it can be transferred on to the entry form.

E	A	H	E	I	N	Z	B	A	K	E	D	B	E	A	N	S			
	C		S										E						
		H		K									T						
B			O		A								S						
		I		M		E							N						
		R			A		T						O						
D			D			R		S					Y						
R			S			G		D					L						
A					C			A		O	T	E	U	S	A	R	O	T	A
T						U		R			C								
S						S				I		E							
U							T				N		Y						
M								A				E		E					
S										R					S				
N											D	R	I	V	E	D			
A																	R		
M	I	N	C	R	E	A	M											I	
L																			B
O																			
C			R	U	O	L	F	E	D	I	R	P	E	M	O	H			

You will find the names of various products listed on posters in this store. You are invited to write them down in the space provided on the left-hand side of this form and then take the form home to try and find the products listed that are hidden among the rectangle of letters.

Well-known brand names of goods may be printed up or down the rectangle of letters. They may also be written across, diagonally or back to front.

When you have found all the products listed, and circled them with a pen, fill in details of your name and address, and attach the form to labels from each of the items listed. Only labels that are stamped with our own stamp will be accepted. These must be securely pinned to the entry forms and placed in the box provided at the store.

The first all-correct entry form drawn from the drum will be judged the winner. The draw will take place at 12 noon on Saturday, 1 May 19 . . . , at Poppy Lane Store, High Street, Cheltenham. The prize for the winning entry is a shopping voucher for £25.

PRINT PRODUCT NAMES HERE

COLMANS MUSTARD   LYONS TEA
HEINZ BAKED BEANS   MIN CREAM
BIRDS CUSTARD   ATORA SUET
ECHO MARGARINE   DRIVE
BIRDS EYE COD STEAKS   HOMEPRIDE FLOUR

```
E A S H E I N Z B A K E D B E A N S K O P
V C A S V T O E A N E R O A T E I K A T I
E A H A K E N A I T R M E I L T N O T M C
B E C O N A I L N O A O R T A S E A E E M
A I N M M T E O A E N R A E N N A R A N O
E A R O A A T T L R E I O B A O T S T C N
D N O D O I R A S T T S A I E Y I F A E C
R A A U S G H G I D A U I F C L A O B A S
A E T N E C O N A L O T E U S A R O T A Y
T A N E T A U A O R M C I N R A S U N L P
S C U E R N O S A N I A E A H S I R E A T
U E A B O A T N T A A N U Y A R O V E W A
M L E I A D O O E A P R E O E A R U N A L
S L P N D A O N R N R O I U D S A N D L S
N O S A Z E N O A E O D R I V E D O W N T
A P I M E R P T M A T A S F A V O R I O A
M I N C R E A M P T T V O A I E A O I W N
L N R E A I V R O I A E T H I D E N D B D
O S A H I F T E C A S T O M H Y R E O S S
C O O R U O L F E D I R P E M O H T R E A
```

Name..
(Block capitals)

Address..

Telephone................................   Date...................

FIGURE 8. Sample entry form

8. Guess How Many Items Sold

This promotion can be run successfully in retail outlets. It makes no difference what the shop sells or how large the establishment is. It is another one that can be operated on a very small budget. In fact, if support is obtained from manufacturers, the cost of this promotion could be nil!

Equipment needed

- A sheet of paper with the answer to the question, concealed inside a sealed envelope.

The promotion

Having selected the item that you wish to promote, you must secretly record the number of units of this product that you have sold over a period of two or three weeks. Then record the answer on a piece of paper and seal it in an envelope. It is vital that this information is shared with no one, as it is so easy for staff to pass the details on to their friends.

Customers who purchase goods valued at £2 or more are asked to guess how many units of the particular product are sold in your shop within the number of days specified and give their answer on the entry forms you provide. The competition item can be anything that is regularly on sale, like a certain brand of tinned food, half-pound packs of butter or anything with a similarly high turnover. In a DIY store, the product chosen might be pre-packed screws or adhesives.

The customer can have any number of guesses, so long as each guess is made with a purchase.

At the end of the competition, the person nearest to the correct number of the items sold wins the prize. If there is more than one all-correct entry, the names are put into a drum and the winning entry is drawn.

Manufacturers are usually pleased to offer financial help

towards the cost of this promotion because for them it is a cheap and easy way of advertising their product.

9. Surprise Vouchers

This is a simple but very effective means of increasing the sale of newspapers, with the added advantage that when customers call to buy their papers they will hopefully purchase other items while in the shop.

The promotion is very cheap to run, costing less than £3 per week to operate, and yet it is a strong favourite with members of the public. The thought of receiving something for nothing has a magic appeal, and newsagents who operate the 'Surprise Voucher' promotion find that customers buy from them rather than the shop down the road which is not offering the same incentive.

Equipment needed

- Vouchers.
- Posters to advertise competition.

The promotion

Twice a week you conceal a voucher inside one of the newspapers and this will entitle the finder to a free copy of that newspaper each day for a period of two weeks. The vouchers are not given to regular customers who have their newspapers delivered but to customers who call into the shop casually.

The voucher can be transferred to various newspapers during the following weeks, until eventually all the different papers you sell over the counter will have had one.

Large posters in your main window and inside the shop are

vital to the success of this promotion. People passing by must understand that they have an opportunity of choosing a newspaper that has the free voucher hidden inside it. Poster advertisement plus word of mouth should soon arouse public interest and support.

It may be possible to obtain a small financial support from all your newspaper suppliers, as the success of this project will benefit them just as much as you. In this case you could offer a larger number of vouchers each day.

10. Lucky Number Draw

This promotion has been run very successfully in various retail outlets, including pubs, garages and shops. Again, it is a cheap and effective promotion, the only material outlay being posters to advertise the venture and the cost of 100 discs.

Equipment needed

- 100 discs, numbered from one to 100.
- A bag, painted jar or other opaque container to hold the discs.
- Two drums to hold entry forms.
- Lined paper to record guesses.
- Posters.

The promotion

Having obtained a receipt for goods purchased, customers write on the back their name, address and telephone number and a guess as to the order in which they think three numbered discs will be drawn from a container at the end of the week. They then place this entry into a drum provided for the purpose.

Each evening, remove all the receipts from the drum and record the name, address, telephone number and three guesses on a separate sheet of lined paper. This means that the winning entry can be clearly identified without having to sift through all the entries at the end of the week. Receipts are then transferred to a second drum and the original drum is left empty for use the next day.

Each Saturday, and at the time advertised, at the busiest time of the day, when there are a number of people around to witness the draw, a customer should be invited to take three discs from the bag without looking inside.

As each disc is drawn from the bag the number is written down. This sequence of numbers should be left on display so that people can check the winning numbers. The numbers on display also often act as an incentive to people to try harder to win the game the next opportunity they get.

Check the list to see if any customer has guessed the correct order of the draw. If there is no winner, then the prize for that week is added to the following week's prize, until the winning sequence of numbers is drawn. When the prize is doubled in this way, a notice to this effect should be on display in the shop window to attract more people to try their luck.

A suitable prize would be a food voucher for £25, though the amount will depend on your budget. All vouchers are to be spent at your store.

11. Know Your Beef Cuts

This promotion has been very successful in attracting customers to butcher's shops and it can be successfully operated in supermarkets where meat is sold.

Equipment needed

- Vouchers (see Figure 9).
- Application forms (see Figure 10).
- Posters to advertise competition.

The promotion

Give customers an entry form and a voucher for every purchase of £1.50 or more made in the shop. When they have collected TWO vouchers they are eligible to enter the competition. On the entry form is a list of beef cuts, a rectangle of letters and a printed outline of a bullock. Competitors have to draw in all the various cuts of meat listed on the diagram in approximately the right size, shape and location.

Having done this, customers then locate the names of the various cuts of meat which are hidden within the rectangle of letters printed on the right-hand side of the entry form. When the name of a meat cut is found, they should draw a circle around the word.

Customers must submit TWO vouchers with their entry form.

The winner is the first person whose name is drawn from the drum with correct answers to both parts of the competition.

The draw should take place on the shop premises on the quietest day of the week to increase trade on that day.

Suitable prizes would be £25 in cash or vouchers for the winners, and cuts of meat for the two runners-up. You could run the competition bi-weekly, and organise a total of six games to give customers further opportunities to win.

Bear in mind that the cost of the prize is based on the retail value of meat sold in the shop. The actual cost of the prize to you will be far less than the value of the prize.

The beef marketing board may help you pay the cost of printing vouchers, entry forms and posters to advertise the promotion in the shop.

As well as placing a large poster in the main window of your shop to advertise the promotion, try to persuade another local shop to advertise your promotion in return for a promise to reciprocate at some future date.

MERCHANT BROS MEAT AND POULTRY	**V**
Main Street, Bovey, Herts.	**O**
KNOW YOUR BEEF CUTS COMPETITION	**U**
A voucher given for every £1.50	**C**
spent in this shop. Collect	**H**
TWO vouchers to qualify for entry into the	**E**
competition.	**R**

FIGURE 9. Sample voucher

Each time you purchase beef to the value of £1.50 or more from this shop, you will be given a voucher. Collect TWO of these vouchers to qualify for entry into a competition to win a shopping voucher for £25.

The competition is in two parts:

1. Look at the names of cuts of meat on the left-hand side of this form. Now look at the outline of the bullock and draw in the appropriate sections to show where the various cuts of meat are found.

2. Try to locate in the rectangle of letters shown, all the names of those cuts of meat listed. The words can be written up or down, right to left, left to right, or even diagonally. Draw a circle around each word that you find.

When both parts of the competition are completed, fill in your name and address below, and return your entry form to this shop (with two vouchers firmly attached), no later than Saturday, 1 June, at 5.30 p.m. The draw for the winner will take place at 12 noon on Monday, 3 June.

FIGURE 10. Sample entry form

KNOW YOUR BEEF CUTS

Cuts of Meat	Name ....
Silverside	
Rump	....
Shoulder	
Chuck Steak	Address ....
Sirloin	
Fillet	....
Flank	
Brisket	....
Fore Rib	
T-Bone Steak	Telephone ....
Leg	
Shin	

```
A C Y N S I L V E R S I D E D E A M P T
R E A O H N E O C A A N I R O M L N O O
R U M D I N A L A S T A F A R M T I Y M
C O M R E D L U O H S T A E M I O O A M
F T E P S I L V E R S E D E B T P L R E
G L T O H U R A K O P L O R A E O R E N
E U A L I R A A N A A L O O N N R I D A
L P E A N O B R I Y H I N A E D C S K I
E D V E D G R O T O A F O T C I L A O M
B I R E R O F T U B N I L E R F O M P I
A V O M O O B O B R I S K E T K A T O H
G I T C H U C K S T E A K E R A U I H O
L K A E T S E N O B T I N K N A L F I N
W I N G R O B U N M E E A E O J I A T O
```

Rump

[83]

12. Win A Prize With Your Name

This competition gives all shoppers an even chance of winning a prize.

Equipment needed

- Printed entry cards or forms.

- A container to hold the entry forms.

- Lined paper.

- 1,000 numbered raffle tickets.

- A drum.

- Posters to display the alphabet and the different numbers which have been allocated to each letter.

- A dispenser to hold the cards or entry forms.

The promotion

As people come into the store, they are invited to take a card from a dispenser which has been placed at the entrance.

The wording on the card invites customers to write down their names in capital letters; there is a maximum of THREE Christian names plus a surname permitted.

Having written their name clearly, customers must then look at a poster which displays each letter of the alphabet and a number, from one to twenty-six, which is allocated to each letter of the alphabet: e.g., $A=1$, $B=2$, $C=3$, etc. They then write down the numbers that have been allocated to each letter in their name, add them up and place the total score in the box provided on the card.

For example, if the above code is used:

TOM SMITH would give the numbers 20 15 13 19 13 9 20 8. Total: 117.

Competitors must remember to write down their name and address on the entry form, together with the date on which the entry was submitted, and each form must be accompanied by a receipt for goods purchased.

The forms are then placed in a drum to await the draw. At the end of the week, at a specified date, time and place, a number will be drawn from a container that holds 1,000 cloakroom tickets, numbered from one to 1,000. The customer who has written down the same score as the number which is drawn from the drum wins a shopping voucher which is redeemable at the store. Should there be more than one winner, the names of the winners are placed into a drum and a member of the public is asked to draw the winning entry.

To enable this promotion to last several weeks, and to maintain the excitement during this period, give the letters of the alphabet different numbers each week or fortnight. Letters given low numbers one week can be given high numbers in the next competition.

Obviously new posters will need to be displayed to give the new alphabet and numerical equivalent for the next game. It is best to give vowels relatively low numbers and save the high numbers for consonants.

To make administration easier, record each name and total score on a separate sheet of lined paper at the end of each day. In this way the winning entry can be quickly checked for authenticity.

It is essential to display the winning number drawn every week on a poster in the shop. You should also display a copy of the previous weeks' alphabets and numerical allocations so that people can check for themselves again whether or not they have won prizes.

Make it known that the management will NOT be held responsible for checking name and number combinations – that is up to each individual – and will not notify winners. This ensures that customers make a return visit to the shop to check whether or not they have won a prize.

Prize winners should have their names displayed in the store as this increases interest in the competition.

13. Split A Thread With A Dart

This competition is especially suitable for attracting people to clubs and pubs and so increasing turnover. Most people cannot resist the challenge of testing their skills, and throwing darts at unusual targets appeals to a wide range of people, not just seasoned darts players!

Equipment needed

- A sheet of chip board, approximately 4 ft × 2 ft, with a black circle, 9 in. in diameter, painted in the centre.

- Strong white thread.

- A litre-bottle of whisky for each week of the promotion.

- A cushion or piece of foam rubber to catch the bottle when it falls.

- Three darts.

- Cloakroom tickets or till receipts.

- A painted jar or other opaque container.

- Posters to advertise the event.

The promotion

Build the equipment needed to play this game (see construction details below and Figure 11).

Decide in advance how long you intend to run the competition. It can continue very satisfactorily over a period of ten to twelve weeks without losing its interest and appeal for customers.

The costs of the promotion are making the equipment, which you can keep indefinitely, buying a litre-bottle of whisky each week and advertising and printing.

Every time customers purchase a drink, if the competition is being run in a pub or club where there is a bar, they are given a till receipt or numbered cloakroom ticket. Players write their name and address on the ticket and put this into a drum. Obviously those who buy more drinks will have a greater chance of getting their name drawn on the night.

At 9.00 each Saturday night, a customer is invited to draw a name from a drum and the person whose name is drawn is invited to throw THREE darts in an endeavour to break the thread which is holding the bottle of whisky. If this person fails to break the thread, a second name is drawn from the drum, and so on.

The game can continue until a player is successful. If the thread is damaged by a dart, a new length of thread must be used before another player can throw. The game must be seen to be fair to all, and everyone must have the same chance of winning the prize.

To make the game last longer, and to create more excitement, you can decide to draw three names only from the drum. If none of the players wins the prize, a new game is started and all the old receipts are thrown away. The three names drawn the following week then have an opportunity of winning TWO litre-bottles of whisky.

Should the prize not be claimed the second week, the game continues to the third week, when SIX names are drawn from the drum, each person playing in the order that their name is drawn.

If the prize is still not won, start a new game, but on this

[87]

fourth week continue to draw names and play the game until somebody wins the prize of four bottles of whisky.

A weekly draw has great appeal and if prizes have not been won the weeks before, the game attracts much more interest and excitement. Ensure, though, that all promises are met and that customers are made aware of the time, place and venue of succeeding games.

It is ESSENTIAL that people who win the chance to throw darts throw them in person. They cannot choose someone else to throw the darts.

If a name is called and the person is not present, they have forfeited their right to play and another name is drawn from the drum. This assures good attendance on the night.

Display on a poster the names of winning contestants and the number of bottles of whisky they won. This keeps the party spirit going and encourages more people to take part.

Construction details for making the split-a-thread dart game

The chip board should be hung in position so that the bottom of the board is 2 ft 6 in. from the floor.

The centre of the circle should be 2 ft 6 in. from the bottom of the board and positioned directly in the centre of the width of the board. The circle should be painted in black to show up the white thread, and should be 9 in. in diameter.

When the board is in position, the centre of the circle should be 5 ft from the floor.

White button cotton is strong and quite suitable for this purpose. It is essential that the thread is tight against the board as it must be taut to be split by a dart. Always ensure that the thread runs right down the middle of the black circle.

It is a good idea to nail two strips of wood of equal thickness across the top and bottom of your board to give it extra depth from the wall and to accommodate the thickness of the bottle.

A piece of foam rubber or a cushion should be placed

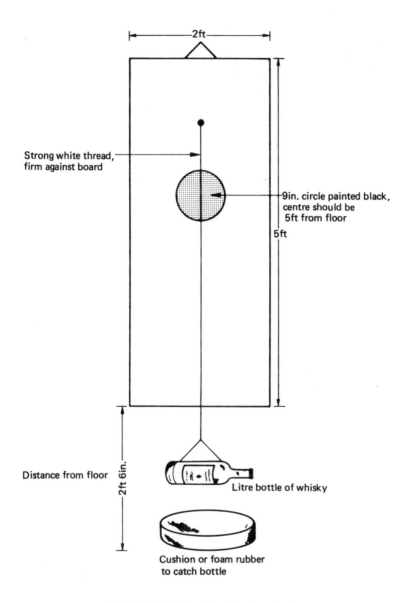

FIGURE 11. Split a thread with a dart

underneath the bottle of whisky to catch it when it falls.

The throwing distance is the same as for a normal game of darts.

Players win the bottle of whisky if they split the thread holding the bottle WITHIN THE BLACK CIRCLE, thus enabling the bottle to drop.

Keep plenty of spare thread to replace any that is damaged by darts.

14. Car Registration Bingo

This is a promotion to appeal to motorists, though shops as well as garages can make use of it. It is a game of luck rather than skill, but people feel a great sense of achievement when they win a prize simply by using their own car registration numbers!

Equipment needed

- Posters showing letters of the alphabet and numbers from one to fifty that have been allocated to each letter.

- Posters showing the number that players must try to match.

- 150 numbered cloakroom tickets in a bag.

- Entry forms (see Figure 12).

- Container to hold entry forms.

The promotion

A number is drawn from a bag that contains 150 numbered cloakroom tickets. That number is written on a poster and put on display.

When customers arrive at the garage, they are given an entry form and are invited to write down their car registration number, name and address. They then look at the poster on display which shows letters of the alphabet and the numerical values that have been allocated to each letter for that week.

Players then add the numbers in their car registration number and those given to the letters, and they record the total figure in the space provided on the entry form. If the figure recorded matches the number on display in the foyer, the player wins a prize.

The letters in the alphabet are given new numbers each week to keep the competition fresh and exciting. In this way the promotion can continue for up to ten weeks without losing its attraction. Obviously, the changing numerical values mean that the same driver can win on more than one occasion.

Each letter of the alphabet should be allocated a number from one to fifty, but be careful not to give two letters the same number. It is easily done. An illustration of one possible sequence is given below.

A	B	C	D	E	F	G	H	I	J	K	L	M
26	13	25	12	34	4	20	11	8	22	15	29	3

N	O	P	Q	R	S	T	U	V	W	X	Y	Z
14	1	50	10	38	40	37	48	5	44	17	7	19

In this example, the car registration GHT 200K gives a total of 85.

To prevent people from making up numbers on their entry forms, it will be necessary for players to submit the log book or insurance certificate as proof of car ownership. In this way the organisers can confirm that the car number is legitimate.

An attractive prize for this promotion is a voucher for free petrol to the value of £10.

[91]

CAR REGISTRATION BINGO
Smith's Garage, West Midlands

Name . . . .
(Block capitals)

Address . . . .

. . . .

. . . .

Telephone . . . . Date . . . .

Car registration number ☐ ☐ ☐ ☐ ☐ ☐ ☐

Numerical equivalent ☐ ☐ ☐ ☐ ☐ ☐ ☐

Total ☐ ☐ ☐

FIGURE 12. Sample entry form

15. Advertising On Mirror Frames

This way of obtaining additional income is especially suitable for hairdressing salons, where people sit in front of the mirrors while waiting for attention.

Equipment needed

- A supply of entry forms or cards approximately 6 in. ×4 in. (See Promotion 7 for details of how to compile the rectangle of letters and lay out the form.)

- Approximately twenty to twenty-five advertisements on

[92]

postcards around each mirror in the shop, the same advertisements around every mirror.

The promotion

Approach local firms and those whose products you sell and
encourage them to advertise their services with you for a fee.
Each firm must write its own advertisement on cards to be fixed
to each mirror in the salon. These should be colourful, eye-
catching and well printed, between twenty and twenty-five
around each mirror. All adverts must be clearly on display: one
must not conceal part of another and none should have any part
concealed from view.

When customers are seated they are invited to take part in
a competition which is held once a month and offers free
hairdressing as a prize. To enter the competition, customers
write down on their application forms the names of all the firms
who have advertised on the cards around the frame of the mirror
in front of them. Having done this, they try to locate the names
of firms, or of products that they sell, which are hidden in the
rectangle of letters on the form. This game is a little more of
a challenge than Promotion 7, because players have to use their
intuition and skill to guess which firm sells the product that
is concealed in the rectangle of letters.

To make the competition more difficult, you could include
only fifteen of the twenty to twenty-five advertisements in the
rectangle and deliberately misspell at least two of the names.

The game helps to pass the time while customers are waiting
in the salon, but they can also take the entry forms home, once
the names of the advertisers have been duly recorded, and look
for the names with the help of their family and friends! When
a word is found, it is circled with a pen.

The entry forms are returned to the shop and placed in the
container provided. The winning entry is drawn at the end of
the month.

Your advertising rate should be £50 per annum, which makes this a very cheap form of advertising. Firms can change the wording of their advertisements every month. Even the names of ones not included in the rectangle are committed to memory, because they are written on the application form and customers have to search to see if they ARE included. When you have assured firms that their names are being absorbed psychologically in this way, you will not be short of customers for your promotion.

Use names of different advertisers and different goods they supply in each new monthly competition. In this way the game will not lose its appeal. With 25 advertisers you will receive an annual income of £1,250. Even if you have to pay for printed entry forms and the cost of prizes, you will still have extra income to enjoy, both from your advertisers and from the influx of customers who come to your shop in the hope of winning a free hair do! If your competitors don't offer this service, you are bound to attract customers.

The prize can be a perm, or two hair cuts, or other free hair treatment to suit your budget. The cost is then kept to a minimum, especially if the free appointments are made for slack periods.

There should be no limit to the number of entries that any one customer can submit, but can obtain an entry form only when they have their hair done in the salon.

At the end of the month, a customer is asked to make the draw. The first all-correct entry wins the prize.

16. Winning Playing Card Combination

This is a popular and very successful promotion that appeals to all members of the public. If used just before Easter or Christmas, the prize could be an attractive hamper.

Equipment needed

- Packs of miniature playing cards, preferably stamped with the firm's name and address.

- Entry forms (see **Figure 13**).

- One or two painted jars or other opaque containers.

- An envelope to contain the slip of paper on which is printed the winning sequence of playing cards.

The promotion

Before the promotion starts, write down a sequence of eight playing cards on a slip of paper and seal this in an envelope. The envelope is then put on display.

Customers are given an application form, and each time they make a purchase they are given the opportunity to take ONE playing card from a container. When they have saved EIGHT or more playing cards, they can submit their entry to the competition.

Customers must write down their guess as to what the winning sequence of playing cards in the envelope might be. The name of each card must be written in sequence in the boxes provided on the entry form. The eight playing cards used are put into an envelope, which must then be sealed and pinned securely to their application form.

At the advertised date, time and place, the envelope containing the slip that shows the winning sequence of cards is opened. The person who has guessed the correct sequence wins. If there is no outright winner, the prize goes to the person who is nearest. Should there be more than one winning entry, the winners are asked to draw ONE playing card from a container. Whoever draws the highest card wins. Runners-up can receive consolation prizes.

[95]

Each time you purchase goods from this store you have an opportunity to pick a playing card from a container that is on the counter. Collect EIGHT or more cards, then write down what you think is the winning combination of playing cards that has been recorded and sealed in the envelope on display in the store.

Here is a clue as to the winning sequence of cards:

1. The first FOUR cards must be of equal value in each suite: for example, four twos or four aces.

2. The second four cards, in the eight-card combination, must follow in numerical order: for example, 1, 2, 3 and 4 of SPADES.

The winning sequence of cards will be revealed here on Monday, 4 August, at 11.30 a.m. If there is more than one winner, a draw will take place and the prize will go to the person who draws the highest card.

To be valid, all entries must be accompanied by the appropriate cards.

one	two	three	four	five	six	seven	eight

Name . . . .
(Block capitals)

Address . . . .

. . . .

Telephone . . . .

All entries must be received by Friday, 1 August 19 . . .

FIGURE 13. Sample entry form

To make the game more exciting without making it easier to win, you can put clues on the entry form. For example:

1. The first four cards of the combination must follow in numerical order: for example, 2, 3, 4 and 5 of HEARTS.

2. The second two cards are of equal value.

3. The third two cards are QUEENS.

To make it easy to determine the winner quickly, it is a good idea to record all the guesses submitted by each player at the end of each day on sheets of lined paper. You can then tell at a glance whether there has been a winning entry, or who has guessed nearest to the correct sequence.

Once the winning sequence of cards is revealed, the slip of paper showing the correct answer must be put on display for all to see, together with the name and address of the winner.

Customers can submit as many entry forms as they like, as long as each one has the right number of cards attached, to prove that purchases have been made.

17. Playing Card Bingo

This is similar to Promotion 16, except that there is no mystery about the combination of playing cards which players must try to find. Players in this game can also take a card from any suite they choose.

Equipment needed

• A poster to display the winning sequence of cards.

- Packs of miniature playing cards, each card stamped with the name and address of the shop.

- Four painted jars or other opaque containers, one for each of the card suites. Each container should state the name of the suite it holds.

The promotion

All playing cards must be stamped with the name of your shop to prevent customers from using their own cards.

When someone buys goods, they are given a receipt and allowed to choose a playing card from one container only. Each container is clearly labelled to state the suite of cards that it holds.

A poster, showing a sequence of EIGHT playing cards, is on display and customers are trying to obtain the same sequence of cards from the containers. Each time they buy goods, they have another chance to pick a card. The winning sequence on the poster should preferably contain two cards from each suite as this prevents a run on one suite.

When customers have collected the eight cards they need, they must submit the cards, together with receipts for each of the purchases made, to get their prize.

Again, the prize could be a hamper, attractively displayed in a basket or box, with a retail value of approximately £40.

The competition goes on until the winning combination has been matched or until the end of the promotion, which should last for a period of six weeks. If no one has won by then, the person who is nearest to an all-correct sequence gets the prize. If more than one person is waiting for a single playing card, then these people can draw from a container and the one with the highest card wins the prize. The others can either claim compensation prizes or have their names put into a drum from which three will be drawn, and these can then receive 'runners-up' prizes.

18. Lucky Straw

This is a fun game for people of all ages who love the idea of an instant prize win!

Equipment needed

- Two painted jars or other opaque containers (sweet jars make excellent vessels for this promotion).

- A container filled with sand.

- A supply of drinking straws cut in half.

- Cloakroom tickets marked 'Sorry, no prize', £1, £1.50, £2 and £3.

- Posters in three different colours, to match three of the coloured cloakroom tickets, ten lucky numbers to be printed on each poster.

The promotion

A numbered cloakroom ticket is put into each straw and the straws are then stuck into a container of sand beside the till.

When customers purchase goods to the value of £2 or more, they are invited to draw a straw from the container of sand. The cloakroom ticket is removed from the straw and if the ticket number matches the number printed on a poster of the same colour on display in the shop, the customer wins a prize worth about £5. This could be a shopping voucher, redeemable at the store.

If the number drawn is printed on a poster that is NOT the same colour as the cloakroom ticket, customers can still win a prize. They are invited to dip into a second sweet jar and draw a second ticket, which will show either the words 'Sorry, no prize' or a sum of money.

60 per cent of the tickets in both jars should be marked 'Sorry, no prize'. Most of the remaining tickets should be marked £1, and prizes could be packets of biscuits or sweets. The remaining tickets should win prizes to the value of £1.50 and £2, with a few at £3 to make the game more exciting.

The promotion can either run for a fixed period, say four to six weeks, or until all the straws have been drawn. Don't forget to display the names and addresses of winners, as this inspires confidence and encourages even more interest in the promotion.

19. The Car Sticker Competition

This promotion can be adapted to suit petrol stations and most types of retail outlet. With good publicity it can become an exciting venture as people join in the fun, and it is certainly an effective way of advertising, as people participating have to look out for car stickers with a firm's name clearly printed on them.

Equipment needed

- Approximately 1,000 printed car stickers which advertise the name of your firm or the name of a supplier.

- Entry forms with narrow lines on which to record car registration numbers and the name and address and telephone number of the competitor. The family car registration number of all those playing the game is also written down in a box provided.

- Notebook for organisers to record all registration numbers of cars which display stickers.

The promotion

The number of car stickers and entry forms you have printed will depend on the number of customers you think will enter the competition during the period of the promotion. It is possible to cover your costs by inviting a supplier to contribute in return for having their name incorporated on the sticker.

As customers purchase goods from your store, they are invited to take an entry form and a car sticker. The sticker is to be placed on the left-hand side of the rear window, where it can be seen clearly.

People are then asked to record the car registration number of any vehicle that is displaying the sticker during the promotion. The more legitimate car numbers they can record, the better their chance of entering the draw to win a prize.

The car number recorded by the most people wins a prize or an entry into a draw. If one registration number is recorded on twenty-five or more application forms by the last day of the competition, the driver of that vehicle wins an opportunity to enter a draw for a substantial and worthwhile prize. All those who have written down on their application form the registration numbers of at least ten of the car numbers that were most frequently seen and recorded will also be eligible for a draw for a worthwhile prize.

To qualify for entry in this second section, the entry form MUST be accompanied by receipts from your store to the value of £5 or more.

No car number can be repeated twice on the same form, even if the vehicle is seen on different days.

Only registration numbers of cars that display the sticker can be entered on the application form. Winning entries must be checked to ensure that all the cars listed are actually taking part in the competition. This is a simple matter as owners' car registration numbers are recorded in a special place on the entry form, and a separate list of these should be made for easy reference.

20. Pick A Key And Win A Prize

This game is simple to operate and it gives members of the public a challenge and a great deal of fun as they try their skill at choosing a key that will open the box! It can be used in any supermarket, shop, DIY store, garden centre or pub. The equipment needed takes up very little space, but the game does need a supervisor who will ensure that it is played fairly.

Equipment needed

- A box with a Yale lock and a container to hold keys (see Figure 14).

- 400 Yale keys.

- A painted jar or other opaque container to hold the keys.

- A slip of paper to be hidden inside the box to show what prize has been won.

The promotion

Each time customers purchase goods to the value of £5 they have an opportunity to pick a key from its container. They must not look inside the box but may take one key for every £5 of goods purchased.

The customer then uses the key to try to open the lock. If it fits, the box will open to reveal a slip of paper which states the prize that has been won. If the key does not fit the lock, it is returned to the container.

It is often possible to obtain 'seconds' from firms that cut Yale keys.

Make sure that only one key in the container fits the lock and opens the door.

All keys should be the same size and shape. Otherwise it is easy for players to tell one from another, and they soon learn which shape key does not fit the lock!

A popular prize for this promotion is a litre bottle of whisky or a shopping voucher valued at £20 which must be redeemed at the store.

Make sure that every person who qualifies is given a chance

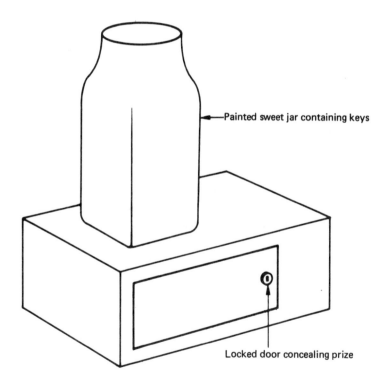

Painted sweet jar containing keys

Locked door concealing prize

FIGURE 14. Pick a key and win a prize

to play the game. Cheerful co-operation on the part of your staff is vital here. If the staff are enthusiastic and helpful, they can ensure a great deal of fun for your customers, who will then return to the shop to buy goods in order to try their luck again.

Never leave the 'Pick a key' equipment unguarded as it has been known for people to tip out all the keys in an attempt to find the right one before the supervisor returned!

21. Meat Freezer Club

Less than 41 per cent of the population are said to have freezers large enough to store meat in bulk. The 'Meat freezer club' can be a popular way to overcome this problem as it gives everyone a chance to buy meat more cheaply in bulk, and it enables people to store their meat in ideal conditions until it is required.

The club has many advantages for butchers too. It offers a simple but very effective way of competing with chain stores and supermarkets. It gives them a quick turnover of meat and it guarantees regular custom. As an extra bonus it also provides a way to use all the space in their freezer! Those who have tried the scheme say that it ensures a degree of security in the business, and this is one of its prime attractions.

Equipment needed

- Large, high-quality plastic bags.

- Metal discs on which the customer's name and address can be printed.

- Lengths of string to tie the bags.

- Either a stock book for each customer to record all the joints of meat that are added to or withdrawn from the container; or record cards in plastic holders, one attached to each freezer bag.

The promotion

Invite people to pay £3 to join your meat freezer club. For this fee they are entitled to buy meat in bulk lots from you, making the meat much cheaper.

Cut the meat into the type of joints required by the customer, then store it in special high-quality plastic bags, which are kept in the shop freezer.

One large bag is reserved for each customer. Each one is tied with string, which also holds a metal disc on which is recorded the customer's name and address. This bag can be hung on hooks from the roof of the freezer, so that it can be found easily when required (see Figure 15).

It is essential to record details of all new stock that is added to the container, as well as any meat joints that are removed. This can be done either in stock books that customers take home with them or on record cards which are kept in plastic containers tied to the customer's freezer bag. It does not matter which system is used.

If customers prefer a record book, then each joint of meat that is placed into the container is recorded in the book. When a joint is removed, it is marked off in the book. Customers sign this book to confirm that they have taken the meat. If this method is used, customers must ALWAYS bring their record books with them if they want to take meat from the freezer. There must never be any doubt about who has taken meat from a customer's container.

As the record cards are kept at the shop, this is a very satisfactory way to keep a check on what meat customers have added to or taken from the container. They sign the record sheet whenever a transaction is made.

You would be well advised to advertise in advance of the commencement of your freezer club. In this way you can assess how many people will be taking advantage of the facility. The £3 membership fee will help pay the cost of advertising, organising and administering the scheme.

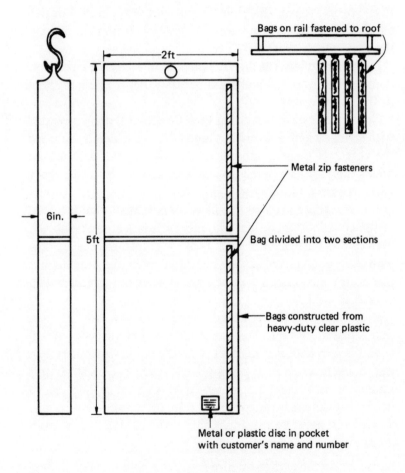

FIGURE 15. Bulk meat freezing unit

[106]

22. The DIY Club

This type of club has become very popular as the cost of professional builders and decorators has continued to rise.

Equipment needed

- Membership cards.
- A wide assortment of electrical and other equipment for hire.
- A monthly newsletter.
- An up-to-date record of the skills and occupations of all members who are willing to do casual work for other members of the club.

The promotion

The public are invited to pay a subscription of £5 to join a DIY club, and £3 per annum thereafter. Membership cards are given out.

Record details of the various skills of your members and then advertise the services they offer to members in need of help with DIY jobs. Plumbers, carpenters, electricians and other tradesmen will help members and each other for a reasonable fee.

Members who have special trades or skills that they wish to sell can also advertise their services at no cost in the monthly newsletter.

Tradesmen who need casual help could also advertise for part-time assistants, and unskilled people who are willing to help professional tradesmen could offer their services in this way. The householder in need of a tradesman will also find this newsletter of interest and value.

It is important to have a large variety of tools for jobs in the house and in the garden on hire for club members. The joining fee should go a long way towards the cost of purchase of hire equipment. You should place a seven-day hire limit on all goods, so that members have a fair chance to hire the items they need for a very small fee.

Aim to attract at least 1,000 members to the club. These will be regular customers, whose membership fees will pay the cost of the newsletter. If you are ambitious, you can improve it, and bring in extra income, by selling advertising space to the many manufacturers of tools and products that are on sale in your shop.

23. Developing A Lunchtime Food And Drink Delivery Service

This sort of delivery service can be very lucrative. It can certainly assist an off-licence to expand in an enterprising and appealing way, but remember that it may be necessary to obtain permission from the local licensing court if you sell beer, wines and spirits, because in some districts you need a special licence to sell liquor in this way.

Equipment needed

- Printed leaflets giving details of the service and the menu available.
- Order books.
- Mini-van to hold large metal food-containers and boxes of bottles.

The promotion

If your shop or off-licence business is situated near an industrial estate, this service will be very popular with employees who do not have canteen facilities and who may have to travel some distance in order to buy refreshments.

First, have an attractive leaflet printed, outlining the service on offer and listing the type of goods for sale, with prices. At the bottom of this leaflet is an order form, to be collected each day from the firms that you visit. The order can then be delivered the following day.

It is obviously important to secure sufficient custom to make the travelling and work involved worthwhile. To begin with you will need to make it clear that the service will be offered only if enough orders are taken each day. Once you get through the initial period, the enterprise is likely to develop quickly when people find out that you are delivering a range of fresh and tasty food and beverages at a reasonable price and the orders will come flooding in. Make the service personal and always ask people what they would like you to provide.

It is possible to equip a small mini-van with boxes to keep the food inside hot and intact. Pies can be kept hot if they are stored in large metal containers that have been filled with polystyrene granules.

To be able to deliver the food within the lunchtime period, and to economise on petrol, you need as many orders as possible within a small area. Once you have delivered, collect the order for the following day and leave more forms for the day after that.

For special occasions, like Easter and Christmas, you could offer discount to customers who have given the most orders during the preceding months.

24. Price-tag Word Game

This is another promotion that involves a word puzzle game, and as customers have to find a range of products for sale hidden

Each time you purchase an item for 50p or more from this store, peel off the sticky price tag and restick it on to one of the spaces below.

When you have collected the fifty price tags in this way, complete the word game and return the form to this store before 11 January 19 . . .

Look carefully at the rectangle of letters and find the names of twenty products that are sold in this shop. The name of each item can be printed either up or down the rectangle, across or diagonally, or back to front. Circle each word with a pen as it is found.

At 12 noon, 2 January, a draw will take place to find the first all-correct entry to this competition. The winner will receive a voucher for £50 to buy goods at this store.

```
C R O W N P A I N T A S E V L E H S E N I P
A H A O E I E R O L E O R I O W A E R T T A
R O U W A R K S C A R S P A R E S E N A A T
T A T B L T I E A H S E A T E A I A E E R E
E R E E B P O R W S E H C N E B E N I P T S
R S V A W L L V L I A R O V I N G W O N R S
S E L L S A O U E L R I S L A Y I N G E A T
S L E E P T A C G V I N A S T O I L L D T E
E D A E L T B O K S N G I T C U W I L R E P
E N A M E E A T H S G I U C O I A N R A T R
D A N D E R S W A L L P A P E R S G O G A A
S C O L T S H O T T A L W I T O I S T S I C
K S V O R C I A E O N I A E U T P I O R W S
C R E O U R C L W B L O C T N E S O R R E R
I E S E L I T G N I L I E C S R E D N A S O
T W O O M M A U O T R E L O I A T O A C O N
S O N R E P A L U T O R T W N T E N T E T N
O L O O T E O P N E S L O O T D O O W C R A
V F R U O R T E W O R T N W A C S R O N I M
E L A N (G A R D E N T O O L S) S A S E N O J
```

Write down the names of all the products that you have found and circled in the rectangle of letters.

1. GARDEN TOOLS	6.	11.	16. . . . .
2.	7.	12.	17. . . . .
3.	8.	13.	18. . . . .
4.	9.	14.	19. . . . .
5.	10.	15.	20. . . . .

Name . . . .
(Block capitals)

Address . . . .

. . . .

Telephone . . . .

Fix your price tag here:

1	2	3	4	5	6	7	8	9	10
11	12	13	14	15	16	17	18	19	20
21	22	23	24	25	26	27	28	29	30
31	32	33	34	35	36	37	38	39	40
41	42	43	44	45	46	47	48	49	50

FIGURE 16. Sample entry form

in a square of letters, manufacturers are usually pleased to help with the cost in return for the advertising they are getting. You could ask either for money towards the cost of the promotion or for prizes.

Equipment needed

- Price tags, printed with the name of the firm.
- Entry forms with printed squares and a word puzzle (see Figure 16).
- A drum to hold all the entry forms.

The promotion

Attach price tags, printed with the name of the firm, to each item for sale at 50p or over in your shop.

Customers have to stick their price tags on to the spaces provided on the entry form. The number of spaces will depend on the value of the range of goods sold in the shop and the average sum of money spent by customers on each visit. A DIY shop may require sale labels marked 50p, while another shop would require labels to the value of £200.

There is then a word puzzle to be completed. Customers must look closely at the rectangle of letters to find the names of products that are sold in the store. The words may be written backwards or forwards, vertically up or down, or diagonally. They must be ringed with a pen when they are found.

All entry forms must be returned to the shop before the given closing date.

The first all-correct entry drawn in public at an agreed date, time and place wins the prize.

The higher the value of tags to be collected, the better the prize should be. Aim for shopping vouchers to the value of at least £25 for a supermarket and £40 for a DIY store. If possible, and if the budget runs to it, you could offer second and third runners-up prizes too.

25. The Gardeners' Club

This is a very popular promotion, especially for garden centres, and it can improve turnover considerably.

Equipment needed

- Membership cards.
- Purchase vouchers, a different colour for each quarter.
- Purchasing cards to record details of each purchase and when it was made.

- Notebook for keeping records of hired equipment.
- A quarterly magazine.

The promotion

The public are invited to pay a £5 subscription to join the gardeners' club, and thereafter £3 per annum.

Every time members purchase goods, details of the sale are recorded on their purchasing card. Members can leave their cards at the store permanently or look after them themselves – if the latter, they must always bring them every time a purchase is made. At the end of each quarter, the totals of all purchases are added together and vouchers are given to the value of 7½ per cent of that amount. These vouchers can be used to buy goods.

To give the gardeners' club extra appeal, offer to sell your members' surplus flower and vegetable plants on a commission basis. You can also operate a hire service for a nominal fee, so members who would not find it economic to buy the tools themselves will come to you. A popular choice of tools for hire would include rotavators, trimmers, hedgecutting devices, electric mowers and saws. Portable cork benches, socket sets, barbecue equipment, carpet-cleaning aids and even ramps for motor cars have proved worth hiring out in the past, but the best way to determine the requirements of club members is to ask them, via a questionnaire. Remember, though, a record must be kept of all goods out on hire, and care must be taken to ensure that a seven-day hire rule is strictly observed. Otherwise you can run into all sorts of difficulties.

Depending on the number of people interested, you might decide to take things further. You could consider producing a quarterly magazine, arranging the occasional lectures and holding quiz evenings and question and answer sessions. Activities like these will keep people both informed and involved in what's going on, and should prove popular.

26. Holiday News Trolley

This is another promotional idea that brings in useful extra income at very little trouble or cost. It can be used in any retail outlet, but it is particularly successful in hairdressing salons and clubs, where people have time on their hands and tend to stop and browse through any leaflets that are around.

Equipment needed

- Trolley (see Figure 17).
- Travel agents who will pay a fee for the privilege of advertising unusual and cut-price holidays to people they would not normally have reached.

The promotion

Have the trolley made, then offer local travel firms the opportunity of displaying their holiday literature on it. Each company could be offered two slots on the trolley for a fee of £100 per annum. If twelve firms each paid this amount to display two leaflets, you would receive £1,200.

The trolley would have space for between twenty and thirty-two brochures, each giving details of different kinds of holiday. Travel firms can change the contents in the display unit as often as they wish. Your customers will find this a very satisfactory way of passing the time: most people like a glimpse of the big, wide world that is waiting to be explored.

So, for less than £2 a week, you are offering a very worthwhile service to travel agents. Your customers are a captive audience with time on their hands and they are not under pressure. These are just the sort of circumstances in which people are likely to absorb information – and hopefully find an unusual holiday, something different that they didn't even know about but would like to try. And the offer of a cut-price holiday can tempt even those who weren't seriously thinking of going away anywhere.

HOLIDAY NEWS TROLLEY

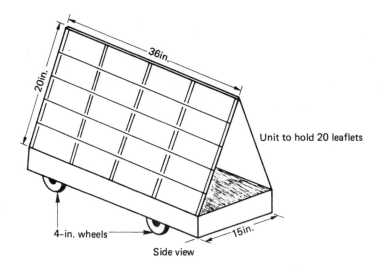

Unit to hold 20 leaflets

4-in. wheels

36in.

20in.

15in.

Side view

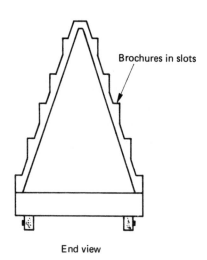

Brochures in slots

End view

FIGURE 17. The holiday news trolley

27. Match The Number

This promotion can be used to advantage in any retail shop or store. It brings in people who are hoping to win something for nothing, and those people who want a prize must first look at the goods on display to find a gift that bears the number they have been given. While looking for one thing, it is anticipated that they will find others that they might like to buy!

Equipment needed

- A minimum of 2,000 leaflets, all numbered, giving details of the promotion.
- Items that are given the same numbers as those on some of the leaflets.
- An inventory showing the prize for each winning number. (This information is kept solely as a check for you so that numbers cannot be transferred from one prize to another by customers who would prefer a more exotic prize!)

The promotion

Have a minimum of 2,000 leaflets printed. These will advertise your firm and explain to people that if they bring the leaflet to your shop and its number matches the number on one of the items on display in the shop, then they will win that numbered item as a prize.

Ten items in the shop should display the same number as ten of the leaflets that have been distributed. The value of the prizes should be approximately £5.

The leaflets can either be delivered door to door or handed to people in car parks and busy shopping precincts in the area. If you and your family cannot undertake this task, then ask a local youth organisation to do the job in return for a donation to their funds.

If customers do not want the item that they have won, they can exchange the prize for another item of a similar monetary value.

A manufacturer or supplier might be prepared to bear the costs of printing if you add their name to the leaflets. It is a good form of advertising for them and their contribution will obviously cut down your outlay considerably.

28. Light The Light

This promotion is cheap and simple to organise and to operate, yet it gives customers a bit of fun as they try their skill at lighting the light.

Equipment needed

- A unit built in plywood, similar to that shown in Figure 18.
- A painted jar or other opaque container which is fixed to the unit.
- 400 ignition keys.
- Old car ignition switch and four keys which operate it.

The promotion

First build the box. It is best to use plywood, which will withstand wear and tear. The unit can then be used many times over the years.

It is possible to obtain ignition keys and switches very cheaply from car breakers. The keys must all be similar in size and shape so that no key feels different from the rest of the keys in the container, and so that the winning keys cannot be identified by touch.

Each time customers buy goods to the value of £2 or more,

they are invited to pick a key from the container on top of the box unit. They then put the key into the ignition switch and try to switch on the light.

If they succeed, they get a refund in full on the goods they have just purchased. If they fail, then they return the key to its container.

Any customer who purchases goods to the value of £10 can select a second key, an extra key being taken for every subsequent £10 spent in the shop.

Should a customer pick two winning keys, give them a shopping voucher, redeemable in the shop, for twice the amount already spent.

As it is very difficult to find four winning keys from 400, the

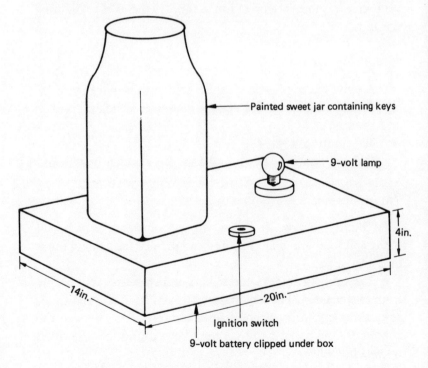

FIGURE 18. Light the light

promotion could go on for a long time without the prize being won. Keys are always returned to the container, so it is a matter of luck if the winning key is drawn. Obviously customers should NOT be allowed to look inside the container. Temptation is great, and someone must supervise the game to ensure that it is played fairly by all.

The names of winners should be prominently displayed on posters inside the shop and in the main window. This arouses interest in the promotion and attracts more customers.

Research has shown that in anticipation of success, people tend to spend more in this competition than they normally would, in the hope of recouping their money. If they win having purchased goods valued at only £2, this isn't much of a prize; but if they make all their purchases in your shop, by spending more their excitement increases and they anticipate a much more valuable prize.

29. Car-sales Advertising

This is a promotion that is especially suited to hairdressing salons, as it gives customers something of interest to do while they are waiting. It is said that the average waiting-time is up to twenty-five minutes in a busy salon; this time can be made to pay.

Equipment needed

- Several A4 folders, preferably with pockets.
- Several A4 sheets of paper.
- A supply of postcard-size adverts.

The promotion

Approach all the local car-sales firms and invite them to submit typewritten descriptions of all the cars that they have for sale. They can give as much detail as they like about each car, and they can use both sides of the A4 sheet. Each firm will give you one copy of their advertising sheet for every folder that you have in the shop. The number will depend on how many customers you can have waiting in the shop at one time.

These advertising sheets can be changed as often as necessary. Information on the sheets should be kept up to date: weekly or twice-weekly the details about sold cars are withdrawn and information about new cars is added. It is the responsibility of advertisers to update their own information and deliver the completed sheets to the shop.

The cost of car-sales advertising would be £100 per annum, making this a cheap but very effective way of advertising for the firms concerned. They have a captive audience with time to relax and absorb what they are reading.

The idea need not be limited to car sales. Consider your clientele and decide what sort of services they might be interested in. You can then approach all sorts of local firms. A charge of £20 per annum, payable in advance, would be reasonable.

30. Lucky Spot Prize

This very simple competition adds a degree of fun and excitement to shopping. The only thing you need is enough space: if people are too crowded together it could be difficult to determine who is standing on the lucky spot.

Equipment needed

- Approximately thirty envelopes, each containing a different detailed route to direct a member of staff to a new lucky spot each day.

- An alarm clock.
- A box to hold the clock and tape to seal the box lid.

The promotion

Twice weekly, set an alarm clock to make it ring at some time during a busy period of the day. Then seal the clock in a box. This ensures that you are the only one to know when the alarm clock is going to ring.

At the sound of the alarm, ask customers to stand still until the lucky prize spot is found. Those people who move about and carry on with their shopping are not eligible to win a prize.

Ask a customer or a member of staff to take an envelope from a pile of about thirty which contain directions on how to find different 'Lucky spots' within the building. The directions might say, for example:

'The lucky winner today is the customer who is standing closest to the corner of the meat freezer that contains the section with the frozen sausages in it.'

An attractive prize would be to offer the customer standing nearest the lucky spot all the goods they already have in their trolley or basket free of charge.

This competition encourages people to buy large amounts of goods in the hope that they will be lucky enough to be standing in the right place when the alarm goes.

It is important to alter the days and times of subsequent 'Lucky spot' events, as this increases the excitement the competition engenders. No one knows WHEN the alarm will ring, but everyone has an equal opportunity of winning the prize of free goods.

By having at least thirty envelopes which look the same and yet contain directions to different spots, you reduce the risk of people guessing correctly which 'Lucky spot' will be selected that day.

[121]

31. Guess The Weight In Potatoes Of The Landlord And Landlady

Most people like to enjoy themselves when they go to a pub for a drink and appreciate any light-hearted fun and entertainment that is offered.

Activities that are a little different help break the ice between strangers and encourage people to relax. Good live entertainment is one way of drawing in the crowds, but competitions and party games are also very popular. People seen to be enjoying themselves are a good sign to new customers, who might well be tempted to become regulars. The following competition is simple to organise and can cause a great deal of mirth as people try to guess the weight of the landlord and landlady without causing offence!

Equipment needed

- A necklace made with potatoes and rope, to be worn by the landlord or landlady to draw attention to the competition and to add a little fun to the event.
- Weighing scales such as those used by farmers to weigh sacks of potatoes.
- Lined paper, with five columns, on which to record guesses.
- An appropriate number of potatoes ranging in size from very small to very large.

The promotion

Customers are invited to write down their guess as to the number of potatoes it would take to make the same weight as the landlord and/or landlady. Guesses can be made and recorded as people order their drinks, but it is more fun if the people to be weighed walk around the bars themselves to encourage everyone to have a go.

Guesses should be recorded on the sheets of lined paper. The first column is for the name of the player; the second is for the weight of the landlord; the third is for the weight of the landlady; the fourth is for the weight of both together; the fifth column is used to record the total number of potatoes needed to match the landlord and landlady's joint weight.

A suitable prize for this competition would be a bottle of wine, a half-bottle of spirits, or cans of beer or lager.

At 10.00 on a Saturday night, the landlord and landlady are weighed in public in the bar, and, once their weight is known, potatoes are weighed out equal to their joint weight and are then counted. The person whose guess is nearest to the correct number of potatoes wins the prize.

The competition can be organised for one specific evening or can continue for two weeks or more before the weigh-in is made. In this case customers would be entitled to an extra guess with each order of drinks that is made.

32. Lucky Birth Date Draw

This is another simple competition which adds a little fun and light entertainment to an evening and creates a welcoming atmosphere in a pub or club. Even newcomers soon feel part of the crowd.

Equipment needed

- Ruled sheets of paper divided into two columns.
- 365 slips of paper, one printed for each day of the year.
- A drum or other container.

[123]

The promotion

Give customers a sheet of paper and ask them to write their name in one column and date of birth in the other. (Their year of birth is not included.)

At the end of the competition, ask someone to draw one of the dated slips from the container, and the person whose date of birth (as recorded on the paper) is nearest to the date drawn wins the prize.

The draw should take place at about 10.00 on a Saturday evening, when the pub is full of people.

Wine, spirits or beer can be given as prizes.

33. Treasure Trail

This is another game which can be used as a very successful means of promoting a pub or club. It is similar to Promotion 30, but the route taken is more complicated, as this adds to the fun in a social setting.

Equipment needed

- An envelope containing detailed instructions on how to follow the trail that leads from point 'A' to the spot where the lucky customer is standing or sitting.
- An alarm clock, hidden in a sealed box or out of view, set to go off at an unspecified time known only to the organiser.
- Measuring tape.

The promotion

No one but you should know the whereabouts of the 'Lucky spot'. Pick a familiar landmark in the pub and write detailed and complicated notes on how to arrive there from some chosen starting-point in the pub. These instructions will be sealed in an envelope until the alarm bell rings to signal that the game has begun.

No one should move once the bell has rung as this disqualifies them from winning a prize. Pick one person to call out the instructions and another to follow them. Both should be fairly lively and outgoing, as the player is going to have to perform some amusing tasks before he or she gets to the end of the trail. For instance, they may have to stand on a chair to measure a space between two marks on the ceiling, or crawl on their knees to measure a distance across the floor. The more inventive the treasure trail notes, the more entertaining and lively the event will be.

Remember that instructions must be VERY precise, however, and a measuring tape should be used where necessary. It is important to ensure that there is no dispute as to the winner, who is, of course, the person closest to the lucky spot selected. Spirits, wine or lager, possibly donated by the supplier, make a very acceptable prize.

34. Drink Measure

This is another game to cause quite a bit of fun on an evening in the pub or club.

Equipment needed

- Tickets or slips of paper on which measurements of liquid are recorded from 1 mm to 130 mm.
- Measuring tape.
- A container to hold the measurement slips.
- An alarm clock sealed in a box.

The promotion

An alarm clock is set to go off at any time after 9.00 in the evening, when the pub is usually full of people. Only the person who is operating the promotion knows when the bell will ring. This element of surprise adds to the excitement of the game.

When the bell rings, people are asked to stop drinking for a few moments while a slip of paper showing a liquid measurement is drawn from a drum or other container.

The person the height of whose drink comes nearest to the measurement of liquid drawn wins. A suitable prize would be a free drink for the winner and a friend, to be consumed that night or on a future visit.

To ensure fair play, the measurement of liquid in the glass must be accurate. Anyone who thinks they have the right height of liquid in their glass must have the drink measured before they can claim the prize. If more than one person has the right height they all win a prize.

If no one has the right height, then the draw is repeated until a winner is found. No one who is playing the game can touch their drink until the measurement of liquid is completed and the winner is known.

Care must be taken to ensure that there is no cheating. Those who have a full glass can be very tempted to drink down the required amount of liquid in order to qualify for the prize!

The game could be repeated twice, or even three times, in one evening to keep the party spirit going!

If a particular brand of drink is chosen for this promotion, it should be possible to obtain sponsorship from the supplier.

35. Guess The Number Sold

This promotion can be used very successfully in pubs or clubs. All you have to do is challenge people to guess how many drinks have been purchased in an evening. Or, as a promotion for the retail trade, ask people to guess how many items of a specified product have been purchased during a stated period.

Equipment needed

- Lined paper.
- A supply of 2p coins.
- A container to hold the coins.

The promotion

Ask people to write down their name, address and their guess as to how many drinks will be sold between certain hours in the evening. This information is recorded on sheets of lined paper which has been ruled into three columns.

Bar staff should put a 2p coin into the container for each drink they sell. If the competition is to run, say, from 9.00 to 10.00, the coin count must start precisely on the stroke of 10.00. Invite customers to supervise the counting of the coins to ensure that the game is played fairly.

The person whose guess is nearest to the correct number wins the prize.

If you want to use this promotion in your shop, remember that till receipts show unrelated sales as well as sales of the item being promoted, so it is a good idea to use coins and a container here as well.

36. Place The Towns

This is a popular promotion which can be run in any type of retail shop.

PLACE THE TOWNS

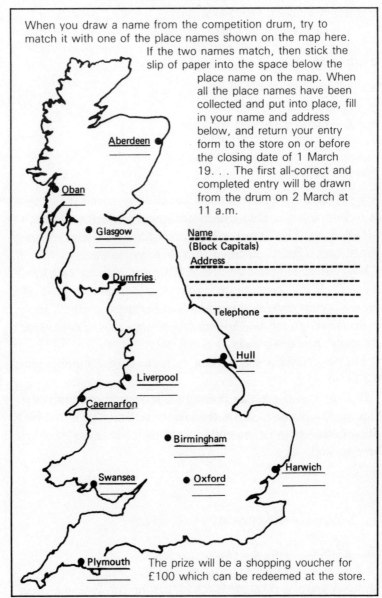

When you draw a name from the competition drum, try to match it with one of the place names shown on the map here. If the two names match, then stick the slip of paper into the space below the place name on the map. When all the place names have been collected and put into place, fill in your name and address below, and return your entry form to the store on or before the closing date of 1 March 19. . . The first all-correct and completed entry will be drawn from the drum on 2 March at 11 a.m.

Aberdeen

Oban

Glasgow

Dumfries

Hull

Liverpool

Caernarfon

Birmingham

Swansea

Oxford

Harwich

Plymouth

Name _____
(Block Capitals)
Address _____
_____
_____
Telephone _____

The prize will be a shopping voucher for £100 which can be redeemed at the store.

FIGURE 19. Sample entry form.

Equipment needed

- Entry forms showing a map of England, Scotland and Wales, with places for at least twelve slips of paper to be stuck under the printed name of a town (see Figure 19).
- At least fifty copies of each place name on the map.
- Slips of paper on which are printed one of at least 2,000 different place names that are not shown on the map.
- Two drums or other containers.
- An envelope to hold every place name slip.

The promotion

When customers purchase goods to a specified amount, they are invited to take an entry form and then draw an envelope containing a name slip from a drum. If the name matches one of those on the map, the slip is then placed in its correct position on the map.

When all the places are covered with matching name slips, the entry form is completed and returned to the organiser, on or before the closing date of the promotion.

This promotion should last for a minimum of ten weeks. All complete and correct entries can then be put into a drum, and on a specified day, time and place, a customer is asked to draw the winning entry from the drum.

A good prize would be a shopping voucher for £100.

37. Surprise Discount And Draw

This promotion has proved very popular, both in the retail trade and in petrol stations. A grocer in mid-Somerset whose trade was seriously threatened by a new superstore used this promotion so successfully that he increased his trade to over

3 per cent MORE than he had been obtaining prior to the opening of the new shop.

Equipment needed

- Slips of paper, some showing the value of the discount that has been won and others printed with details of another draw (read on for details).
- Envelopes to hold the messages.
- Two drums.
- Notebook.
- Posters giving names and addresses of winners, and amounts of discount received.

The promotion

Customers who spend a specified amount in the store are invited to take an envelope from the drum. Inside they will find a slip of paper that tells them how much discount, if any, they have won. The amount of discount will range from 50p upwards, but obviously there will be more slips showing the lower amounts.

If a customer wins discount, this can either be refunded immediately or deducted from the bill on a future visit to the shop. Those who win a discount must write their names and addresses in the notebook provided, and the amount they have won is recorded. This information is then put on a poster to let the public know how many winners there have been and what sums of money have been won.

If the poster is placed in a window, it will attract passers-by. If a second poster, showing the same information, is displayed near the till, it encourages people to return to the shop more often, in the hopes of winning a prize.

Most of the slips drawn from the drum will contain the message 'Sorry, but you have not been successful this time', but on the back of the slip there will be details of another competition (see Figure 20).

Sorry you have not been successful this time, but please retain this slip. When you have collected ten, you are entitled to enter a free draw for a shopping voucher for £10.

Put the slips into one of the envelopes, seal it down firmly and write your name, address and telephone number clearly on the outside.

All envelopes are to be put into the drum provided and entries must be received before the closing date of the competition, on 31 March 1986.

The draw will take place on 2 April 1986.

FIGURE 20. Details of free draw to be printed on all 'sorry' slips

38. Discount Alarm

This promotion is easy to organise, simple to administer, cheap to operate and fun to play!

Equipment needed

- An alarm clock.
- A box to hold the clock.
- A one-hour timer.

The promotion

Each day of the week, set the alarm to go off at a different time. Only the organiser should know the exact time the bell will ring. So that it does not last for too long, do not wind the clock fully. Set a timer to ring precisely one hour later.

From the moment the bell rings, every customer who

[131]

purchases goods to the value of £5 or more is entitled to 7 per cent discount.

It is essential to make it clear to customers that the 'Happy hour' will stop as soon as the alarm bell rings again. When it does, only the person then being served at the till can receive the discount and nobody else.

39. Lucky Discount Day

This promotion has been used very successfully by many petrol stations. Motorists are attracted by the idea of receiving discount on their petrol even though they do not know in advance which day of the week has been selected as 'Lucky discount day'.

Equipment needed

- Eye-catching posters to advertise the promotion to passing motorists.
- A card, approximately 12 in. ×6 in., stating the following in bold print:

**TODAY IS LUCKY DISCOUNT DAY. CONGRATULATIONS!
YOU ARE ENTITLED TO 5% DISCOUNT ON ALL PURCHASES TODAY.**

- Poster to show which were the 'Lucky discount days' on previous weeks.

The promotion

For a period of, say, three months, choose a different day at random each week. This will be known as 'Lucky discount day'.

Motorists will not know which day has been selected until they enter the shop to pay their bill and see the printed card, which you should put on the counter, near the till. Everyone who spends over a certain amount is entitled to discount on all their purchases that day, and this will encourage customers to buy other items from your shop.

40. Match The Letters

This promotion can be used in any branch of the retail trade and in fact works very well as a joint promotion between two firms (as long as they are not in competition with one another), widening its scope and so making it even more attractive to the consumer.

Equipment needed

- Small cellophane envelopes.
- Self-adhesive letters of the alphabet.
- Entry forms..
- Two drums.

Join forces with at least one other firm

To organise a joint promotion, find a firm that sells different products yet attracts the same customers. For instance, a bookshop that sells books for children could link up with a shop that sells children's clothing or toys. Alternatively, two petrol stations that are not in the same area and so are not in competition with one another could join forces to share the cost of the promotion.

The advantages to both firms are obvious: you can share the cost of administration and advertisement, and reach twice as many customers.

The promotion

Each time customers enter the shop, give them a competition

entry form on which is printed either the name of the shop, or, if it's a joint promotion, of the two shops, or a product that they sell. You should use between fifteen and twenty letters of the alphabet.

When someone spends £5 or more, invite them to draw a small cellophane envelope from a drum. In this envelope is a small self-adhesive letter, which must be stuck on to a matching letter in the appropriate place on the entry form.

When each letter of each word is covered, customers fill in their name and address, and return the card to the shop before the closing date of the competition. The prize could go to the first all-complete entry received each month or alternatively you could have a draw at the end of the promotion to find the winning all-complete entry.

This promotion will run effectively for a period of nine months and if two firms are involved, the joint costs are minimal.

41. Win A Cycle

Every child loves the idea of owning a bicycle, and since children tend to be very good at 'persuading' parents to buy things for them, this promotion has a lot going for it!

Equipment needed

- Printed entry forms, numbered in consecutive order (see Figure 21).
- Lined sheets with five ruled columns.
- A box to hold application forms.
- Surveyor's chalk.
- A long wooden ruler.
- A sheet of card on which to record the measurements.
- A cycle as a prize.

The promotion

To make the promotion as economical as possible, approach a cycle dealer or manufacturer and ask for a large discount on the cost of the cycle. You can offer the firm the following promotional benefits.

1. You will be advertising the prize bicycle and the name of the firm supplying it at the same time that you advertise your promotion.
2. You will be displaying the bicycle in the shop, so that members of the public can see the bike and inspect it thoroughly.
3. You will be leaving leaflets to advertise the virtues of the bike in the shop premises.

This form of advertising often encourages people to buy the item, even if they are not lucky enough to win it as a prize.

Draw chalk marks on both sides of each wheel, using surveyor's chalk, as this will not wash off if it rains on the day that the cycle is ridden.

All customers who spend £2 or more in the shop are invited to take a numbered entry form and make their guesses in the columns provided. Each person must guess what the height of each of four chalk marks on the wheels of the cycle will be after it has been ridden along the road for three minutes. The guesses to record are the height of the mark on the left-hand side of the front wheel, on the right-hand side of the front wheel, on the left-hand side of the back wheel, and on the right-hand side of the back wheel. Customers then fill in their name and address, and place the form in the box provided.

At the end of each day, the number of each entry form and the four guesses made are transferred to sheets of lined paper (see Figure 22). This makes extra work, in the short term, but it will be much easier in the end to find a winner simply by looking down a comprehensive list instead of having to search through the answers on hundreds of entry forms.

As long as the number of the entry form is shown, there is no need to write down the name and address of each person who submits an entry form. Forms must be kept in numerical order so that the winning entry can easily be removed.

At the close of the competition, a member of the public is asked to ride the bike for a period of three minutes. The four measurements are then taken using a wooden ruler that is the same height as the wheels of the bicycle. The correct measurements are recorded on a sheet of card, which is signed and dated in front of witnesses. Two witnesses should also sign the card to confirm that the information is correct and that the measurements were fairly taken.

The winner is the person who has guessed the heights of all four chalk marks correctly to the nearest 1/10th of an inch. If no one makes an accurate guess, the person who guesses nearest to the correct measurements wins.

Guess the Heights of the Chalk Marks on the Tyres of a Cycle after the Cycle Has Been Ridden for Three Minutes

The person who guesses correctly wins the bike.

Entry Form No.	Name	Address	Left Front	Right Front	Left Back	Right Back
1	P. Sterrett	1 Main Road, Birmingham	6½″	12¾″	5⅜″	9¼″

FIGURE 21. Sample entry form

Left Front	Right Front	Left Back	Right Back	Entry Form No.
6½	12¾	5⅜	9¼	1

FIGURE 22. Details transferred from entry form on to lined sheets

42. Locate British Towns And Villages

This promotion is not unlike Promotion 36, but it offers even more of a challenge, needing research and a degree of skill if customers are to locate the places in question.

Equipment needed

- Approximately 20,000 paper slips which name twenty towns or villages that exist in mainland Britain.
- Approximately 20,000 slips of paper on which are printed names of places that do not exist.
- Envelopes for each paper slip.
- A detailed map of Europe.
- A detailed map of Great Britain.
- Entry forms showing a map of Great Britain.

The promotion

When customers purchase goods for £2 or more, they are allowed to pick a small envelope from a drum. This envelope will contain a slip of paper showing a place name which may be either real or fictitious. Some of the actual place names should be well known, others less well known. A detailed map of Britain will show you many good-sized towns that fit the bill.

When choosing place names of towns and villages that do not exist, consult a good map of Europe to find places that sound like towns and villages in Britain: for instance, Halden in Norway, Rostock in Germany, Stolbey in Russia. You will find many more.

If customers think the place name drawn is real, they must draw a small circle in red pen at the exact spot on the map to show where the town or village is situated.

They then place completed entry forms into an envelope, together with the place name slips they have collected, and write their name and address on the front of the sealed envelope. Envelope and contents are returned to the organiser on or before the closing date of the competition.

At the end of the promotion, which could be of ten weeks' duration, check all the entries to ensure that the names placed on the map are reasonably close to their actual locations and that each place name is accompanied by the slip showing the same name of the town or village.

If there is more than one winner, select the entry with the most accurate locations marked. If you still cannot find an outright winner, then hold a draw.

A prize of a shopping voucher worth £100 will attract many entries. Manufacturers could be encouraged to sponsor this competition if the product they sell is promoted and sold as a condition of entry into the competition. In this case name the competition after the sponsor: for instance, 'HARPERS LOCATE THE TOWNS COMPETITION'.

People can submit as many entry forms as they wish, provided each form is accompanied by the appropriate paper slips.

43. Bingo Date And Time

This simple promotion has definite public appeal. You're not asking for any great effort from your customers, but the time they choose to make a purchase will determine whether or not they win the prize.

Equipment needed

- Slips of paper on which are printed days of the week that the shop is open.
- A bag or other container for these slips of paper.
- Enough slips of paper on which to record hours and minutes of the working day to cover every hour that the shop is open during a working day.
- A drum or other container for these slips.
- A box or other container to hold the receipts.
- Lined paper.
- Poster to display information about winners.

The promotion

When customers buy goods, they write down their name and address and the time at which they completed their purchase on the till receipt. The name and the time is also recorded on a sheet of lined paper for easy reference.

The till receipts for each day of the week should be kept separately, so that you can easily find the receipt for the winning customer that day at the close of the competition.

The promotion might start on a Monday. If so, the following Monday ask a customer to draw a slip of paper from each of the two containers, one to give a day of the week, the other the time. The winner is the customer whose till receipt shows they were buying goods at the time in question. If no one purchased goods on the time and day drawn, the slip showing nearest to this time wins the prize.

Display the winner's name and the time of the transaction on a poster, then start the competition again for the next week.

Pick the prize that will attract the most business to your store. Goods or vouchers are popular. The promotion can continue for several weeks and retain its appeal if there is a worthwhile prize to be won.

44. Spin The Disc Discount

This exciting promotional venture is ideal for use at petrol stations, and you will find that drivers, hoping to get discount off the price of their petrol, come back week after week. One garage operator found the scheme so successful that he maintained it for sixteen months, claiming that while it was in operation, his turnover increased by 17½ per cent.

The promotion is equally successful in shops. One garden centre ran it for two years. The operators claimed that it attracted customers away from their rivals, two miles away, as, although prices were comparable people preferred to come to their shop in the hope of winning a discount on goods.

The amount of discount offered depends on the amount of business you wish to attract.

Equipment needed

• A disc, 8 in. or more in diameter, divided into at least six sections with each section numbered or marked with monetary bands: i.e., £5–£8, £8–£11, £11–£14, and so on. NB: The disc must be mounted on a balanced spindle so that it rotates freely and has no set stopping pattern.

The promotion

If the promotion is to be used in a petrol station, divide the disc into sections equal to the number of petrol pumps on the forecourt (as long as there are six or more): so, for six pumps sections should be marked from one to six in consecutive order.

Customers who have purchased petrol to the value of £5 or more can spin the disc. If it stops at the number of the pump from which they have just obtained petrol, they win £1 discount.

If the promotion is to be used at a retail outlet, the discs can be divided into any number of sections.

Customers who have purchased goods to the value of £5 or more can spin the disc. If, and only if, it stops on the section that states the amount that has been spent, e.g., £8–£11, then they win £1 discount.

Remember that the customer will have at best a five to one chance of winning the prize. Bear this in mind before deciding how much discount to offer.

45. Match The Coins

Equipment needed

- A selection of coins (about forty in total) of each denomination: 2p, 5p, 10p, 20p, 50p and £1.
- A large painted jar or other opaque container.
- A sheet of hardboard, 2 ft square, painted a bright colour.
- One coin of each denomination, to be stuck firmly to the

hardboard with the date facing upwards so that it can be clearly seen by customers.
- Poster explaining competition to the public.

The promotion

Every time customers buy goods to the value of £5 or more, they are invited to dip their hand into a jar that contains coins of various denominations. They pick out one coin, and if the date on it matches the date on the coin of the same denomination stuck on a board on display, then they win a prize.

Make sure that at least one coin of each denomination in the container shows the same date as the coin of the same denomination displayed on the board, so that customers have a fair chance of winning.

You could offer a prize of a shopping voucher to be spent at your store if anyone matches up all five coins, or a shopping voucher for a lesser amount if anyone matches up four of the five.

The value of goods to be purchased before a customer is eligible to play the game can be varied to suit your situation. This also applies to the value of the prize.

46. The Lucky Straws Competition

This promotion was first attempted by a gentleman I knew who owned a grocery shop. He was suddenly faced with competition from a superstore which had opened two miles away, and his turnover dropped dramatically by 41 per cent.

At first he extended his opening hours, but the extra cost in wages only added to his problem. Then he enlisted the help and support of members of his family, but the quarrelling and bickering that resulted, as family members disagreed over who was doing their fair share, made him feel very disheartened; especially as even with his family's help profits were still 7 per cent down.

Finally, on my advice, he decided to run the 'Lucky straws' promotion. He was not convinced that it would work, but within seven weeks he had improved his turnover by 20 per cent and within three months he was within 6 per cent of his pre-superstore turnover.

During this time he did his homework and found, to his surprise, that if people purchased £30 of goods from the superstore they were making a saving of only £2.70. He displayed a poster on his window to outline the difference in prices between goods purchased at the superstore and goods purchased in his own shop, and this information, together with his 'Lucky straw' promotion, gave a further boost to his sales.

The grocer kept this promotion going for many years, although he did change it slightly to maintain customer interest. Strangely enough, it never seemed to lose its appeal, either for him or his customers, and he always managed to persuade the manufacturers and suppliers of goods that he sold to donate out of the ordinary prizes.

Equipment needed

- Boxes of drinking straws, each straw to be cut into two, three or four sections.
- A container of sand at each check-out point.
- Slips of paper printed with the following:
  a. Sorry, you have been unsuccessful this time.
  b. You have won £2 discount on goods just purchased.
  c. You have won a shopping voucher for £5 which can be used on your next purchase at this store.
  d. You have won the special prize for this month.

The promotion

When customers purchase goods of £2 or more, they are invited to take a straw from the container of sand. In the straw is hidden a slip of paper on which is printed the prize, if any, that has been won.

There are many 'Special prizes' that can be given. The big firms that supply goods to your shop or the manufacturers can be persuaded to offer prizes in return for advertising their products. One good prize is the offer of a three months' supply of a particular product IF this item is included in the shopper's basket of purchases when they make the draw.